Christmas

Christmas

The Annual of Christmas Literature and Art

FOUNDED BY RANDOLPH E. HAUGAN, EDITOR VOLUMES ONE THROUGH FIFTY

Volume Fifty-two

Augsburg Publishing House
Minneapolis, Minnesota

Table of Contents

Editorial staff: Leonard Flachman, Karen Walhof, Jennifer Fast; Allan Mahnke, music.

The Christmas Story

ACCORDING TO ST. LUKE AND ST. MATTHEW

ILLUSTRATED BY PAT BARGIELSKI

And it came to pass in those days that a decree went out from Caesar Augustus that all the world should be registered.

This census first took place while Quirinius was governing Syria.

And all went to be registered, everyone to his own city.

And Joseph also went up from Galilee, out of the city of Nazareth, into Judea, to the city of David, which is called Bethlehem, because he was of the house and lineage of David, to be registered with Mary, his betrothed wife, who was with child.

And so it was, that while they were there, the days were completed that she should be delivered.

And she brought forth her firstborn son, and wrapped him in swaddling cloths, and laid him in a manger, because there was no room for them in the inn.

And there were in the same country shepherds living out in the fields, keeping watch over their flock by night.

And behold, an angel of the Lord stood before them, and the glory of the Lord shone around them, and they were greatly afraid.

6

7

And the angel said to them, "Do not be afraid, for behold, I bring you good tidings of great joy which will be to all people.

"For there is born to you this day in the city of David a Savior, who is Christ the Lord.

"And this will be a sign to you. You will find a babe wrapped in swaddling cloths, lying in a manger."

And suddenly there was with the angel a multitude of the heavenly host praising God and saying: "Glory to God in the highest, and on earth peace, good will toward men!"

And so it was, when the angels had gone away from them into heaven, that the shepherds said to one another, "Let us now go to Bethlehem and see this thing that has come to pass, which the Lord has made known to us."

And they came with haste and found Mary and Joseph, and the babe lying in a manger.

And when they had seen it, they made widely known the saying which was told them concerning this child.

And all those who heard it marveled at those things which were told them by the shepherds.

But Mary kept all these things and pondered them in her heart.

And the shepherds returned, glorifying God for all the things that they had heard and seen, as it was told to them.

Now after Jesus was born in Bethlehem of Judea in the days of Herod the king, behold wise men from the East came to Jerusalem, saying, "Where is he who has been born King of the Jews? For we have seen his star in the East and have come to worship him."

When Herod the king had heard these things, he was troubled, and all Jerusalem with him.

And when he had gathered all the chief priests and scribes of the people together, he inquired of them where the Christ was to be born.

And they said to him, "In Bethlehem of Judea, for thus it is written by the prophet:
'And you, Bethlehem, in the land of Judah,
Are not the least among the rulers of Judah;
For out of you will come a Ruler
Who will shepherd my people Israel.'"

Then Herod, when he had secretly called the wise men, determined from them what time the star appeared.

And he sent them to Bethlehem and said, "Go and search diligently for the young child, and when you have found him, bring back word to me, that I may come and worship him also."

When they had heard the king, they departed; and behold, the star which they had seen in the East went before them, till it came and stood over where the young child was.

When they saw the star, they rejoiced with exceeding great joy.

And when they had come into the house, they saw the young child with Mary his mother, and fell down and worshiped him. And when they had opened their treasures, they presented gifts to him: gold, frankincense, and myrrh.

And being warned by God in a dream that they should not return to Herod, they departed for their own country another way.

And when they had departed, behold, an angel of the Lord appeared to Joseph in a dream, saying, "Arise, take the young child and his mother, flee to Egypt, and stay there until I bring you word; for Herod will seek the young child to destroy him."

When he arose, he took the young child and his mother by night and departed into Egypt, and was there until the death of Herod, that it might be fulfilled which was spoken by the Lord through the prophet, saying, "Out of Egypt I have called my son."

But when Herod was dead, behold, an angel of the Lord appeared in a dream to Joseph in Egypt, saying, "Arise, take the young child and his mother, and go into the land of Israel, for those who sought the young child's life are dead."

And he arose, took the young child and his mother, and came into the land of Israel.

The Christmas Crib

RON KLUG

In the United States it is called the manger scene or nativity set. In France, the *crèche*. In Germany, the *Krippe*. In Italy, the *presepio*. In Spain, the *nacimiento*. In Latin America, the *pesebre*.

Throughout the world, wherever the gospel has been proclaimed, artists and craftspersons have fashioned visual representations of the first Christmas. Using clay, wood, glass, metal, straw—whatever material was at hand—and drawing on their own artistic heritage, they have created visible symbols of the Christmas story. In many places interesting customs, by which the people could express their devotion to the baby Jesus, have developed around the manger.

Who created the first nativity set? When and where was it made? The answer to those questions lies shrouded in the mists of history. Some say that as early as the eighth century—or even the fourth—representations of the baby Jesus with Mary and Joseph were placed near the altars of Italian churches. We know that in 1291 Arnolfo da Cambio carved freestanding figures of the holy family for a chapel of the basilica of Santa Maria Maggiori in Rome.

We also know that a realistic representation of the Christmas scene was popularized by St. Francis of Assisi in the 13th century. In December 1223 Francis had withdrawn for a time from the duties and responsibilities of his rapidly growing order of Poor Friars. In a small hermitage near Greccio he spent his time in prayer, and now he wanted to relive the birth of Christ so that he himself might become more Christlike. Francis wondered how he could make this event come alive again, for himself and others. He felt that, if people would really understand how God became poor for their sakes, their hearts would be so filled with gratitude that they would gladly share with the poor and the hungry, and even give their animals an extra portion of hay.

According to Francis' idea, Giovanni Velita constructed a life-size stable of rough wood at Francis' mountaintop retreat. Inside was a manger filled with hay. Behind it were tethered a live ox and donkey. Nearby stood a simple altar, for the celebration of the Christmas mass.

The people gathered before the stable on Christmas Eve, and their voices rang through the forest as they

This *pesebre*, or manger scene, is from Mexico. The pieces in the *pesebre* are fashioned from clay and then painted. The *pesebre* commands a central place in Mexican homes throughout the season of Christmas. "Feliz Navidad," the Spanish version of "Merry Christmas," is translated "happy nativity."

This crèche from Italy has been carved by the famous Amri artisans. Each piece exhibits elaborate detail in the clothing and facial expressions. Soft, muted colors contribute a richness and serenity to this manger scene.

joined in an ancient Christmas hymn. At the simple altar the Christmas mass was celebrated. Francis, serving as deacon, sang the Christmas gospel. With a strong clear voice he sang out, "And she brought forth her firstborn son and laid him in a manger." Then Francis preached on the wonders of the little child of Bethlehem. His preaching was so vivid that later his friend Giovanni reported that he saw "a child lying in the manger lifeless, and he saw the holy man of God go up to it and rouse the

child from deep sleep. This vision was not unfitting, for the child Jesus had been forgotten in the hearts of many; but by the working of his grace he was brought to life again through his servant St. Francis."

The villagers were so impressed by this re-creation of Jesus' birth that the event was repeated each year. Soon the custom spread to other Italian towns. By the 14th and 15th centuries the nativity set or *presepio* was popular throughout Italy.

At first these nativity sets, carved from wood or modeled in wax or clay, were simple. But as time went on they became increasingly elaborate. In addition to the holy family, the shepherds with their sheep and dogs, and the angel messengers were added. Then came the Wise Men, often richly dressed as kings, followed by their retinue of servants and beasts of burden. To these basic elements other figures were added, representing Italian villagers thronging to the manger or working at their trades—baking, fishing, farming, or building.

This development reached its peak in the 17th and 18th centuries, when whole castles or towns with their surrounding countryside were constructed—always with the Christ child at the center as a reminder of God's presence with his people in the midst of their daily life.

One person responsible for the popularization of the Christmas crib was the Bourbon king, Charles III. He was fascinated by mechanical things, and in 1760 he personally constructed an elaborate manger scene in his castle in Naples. The setting was 40 feet wide and 125 feet deep. It contained 500 wax figures of people and 200 animals. The king himself fashioned some of the figures and accessories, while the queen and her ladies-in-waiting sewed clothes for the figures from velvet and lace.

The nativity set became a popular art form; some of the most skilled artists and craftspersons created unique and lively figures of great beauty and charm. Examples of these 17th and 18th century Italian nativity sets can be seen in some of the great museums of the world.

The Museum of San Martino in Naples houses many of the best of them, including the Cucciniello *presepio* which features 162 human figures, 80 animals, 28 angels, and 450 accessory pieces.

The Metropolitan Museum of Art in New York has an 18th-century Neapolitan nativity set presented by Loretta Hines Howard. Each year the museum exhibits the delicately molded terra cotta figures on a massive Christmas tree. The holy family is stationed at the base of the tree, with the shepherds to the left and the magi to the right. Suspended above them on the tree are nearly 100 angels and cherubs.

In the Italian churches, where many of the fine *presepio* were displayed, special festivities took place around the manger. One of the most famous is at the church of Ara Coeli in Rome. Here is an elaborate repre-

Both of these manger scenes are crafted from wood. The top photo shows a crèche from India made from wooden printing blocks. Below, a crèche from Ireland is pictured. The figures in the crèche are patterned after illustrations in *The Book of Kells*, an early ninth century book containing the four Gospels printed in Latin. The book features elaborate illuminations and decorations in beautiful color.

sentation of the baby carved from wood and studded with jewels. All through the Christmas season children and adults crowd in to see the *bambino* lying in the manger. On a wooden platform erected before the manger, boys and girls recite short speeches or poems in honor of the infant King. On the octave of Epiphany the *bambino* of Ara Coeli is carried in procession to the Capitoline Hill, where a priest raises the statue high to bless the Eternal City and its children.

While these elaborate nativity sets were being created for Italian churches and palaces, families began to set up simple manger scenes in their homes. The more prosperous people could buy costly sets created by famous artists. These became family heirlooms to be treasured for generations. But even the poorest families could create their own Christmas crib or buy inexpensive figures made from plaster or papier-maché.

Today skilled Italian craftspersons still create exquisite nativity sets from alabaster, ceramics, wood, or blown glass. These find their way into homes throughout the world.

From Italy the manger tradition spread into France. In 1316, Pope John XXII, then in residence at Avignon, brought the idea to Provence in southern France. Around 1800, peddlers from Naples traveled to southern France to sell plaster images of saints. These Italian images inspired the French to make their own figures called *santons* or "little saints." The French *santonniers* created not only the biblical characters, but also standard figures such as the fisherman, the baker, the fishmonger, the hunter, or the knifegrinder. The molds for these characters were highly valued and passed on from one generation to another.

Whole families became involved in making *santons*. One member kneaded the clay. Another pressed it into the mold. Another prepared the mold for casting. Still others painted the cast figures.

Santons are still sold today in open-air markets in Marseilles and Nice. A few days before Christmas the French children gather holly, laurel, lichens, and moss to arrange for the crèche. They may create a cave or use flour for snow. The crèche is set up with all the figures except the Wise Men, who are added on January 5, the eve of Epiphany. Above the crèche three candles may be set to symbolize the Trinity.

The crib tradition also spread to southern Germany. Here in the 14th century a popular Christmas custom developed in connection with the *Krippe*. This was the practice of cradle-rocking or *Kindelwiege*. A cradle containing a representation of the Christ child was set up in the church. In the Christmas service the clergy and choir boys took turns rocking the cradle and singing lullabies to the baby, while the others danced around the cradle. Later members of the congregation also

The *retablo* has a long history. When Spanish Conquistadores brought their religion to the Peruvian Indians, the Peruvians built *retablos* as gifts to this God. Today in one area of the Andes, *retablistas* still construct these boxes, depicting life in the villages. At Christmas, nativity *retablos* are popular.

came up to take turns rocking the baby. They would join in singing Christmas carols like this one:

Lasst uns die Kindlein wiegen
Das Herz zum Krippelein biegen.

Let us rock the little Child
And bow our hearts before the crib.

Another peculiarly German innovation was the pyra-

Artisans around the world use clay for fashioning crèches. In France (top) clay is pressed into molds. The resulting figures, *santons*, are fired and painted. This crèche includes a drummer, a peasant woman, a woman carrying baskets, and a man with a bundle of sticks, in addition to the holy family and Wise Men. In Colombia (bottom), the clay is shaped by hand and left in its natural color.

This crèche from Poland is constructed from cardboard and brightly colored foil—a beautiful castle for the newborn King! Notice the figures of the holy family drawn on paper, positioned at the bottom center of the building.

figures known all over the world. Some families work at wood carving the year-around. Boys in their teens become apprentice wood-carvers and devote years of study to continue the tradition of carving figures for the *Krippe*.

In Germany today other nativity sets are made from hand-sculptured clay, lead crystal, pewter, and fine porcelain, like the famous Hummel figurines.

In the 17th and 18th centuries, the nativity set moved to Spain and Portugal, where it is called the *nacimiento*. In the Spanish tradition the baby often is depicted with his hand raised in blessing. At Christmastime the Christ child is carried to every room of the house to bless it.

The Christmas crib also made its way to northern Europe, although there it tended to be overshadowed by the Christmas tree.

One curious form it took in England was the "kissing bunch." Wooden hoops were covered with evergreen boughs and hung from the ceiling. Inside the hoops, figures of Mary, Joseph, and the Christ child were suspended. From the bottom of the "kissing bunch" hung a sprig of mistletoe!

In the Scandinavian countries manger sets are made of wood and straw, often in contemporary designs. In Sweden, for example, stylized straw figures are typical.

When European settlers came to America, they brought along the Christmas crib and its traditions.

Among these immigrants were the Moravians who settled in and around Pennsylvania. They referred to the manger set as the *Putz*, from the German word *putzen*, meaning "to decorate." In addition to the central manger the *Putz* might include farms with animals, a village, bridges, even toy trains. At Christmastime Moravian families still gather around the *Putz* to hear the age-old Christmas story.

mid from the Erzgebirge region of East Germany. The holy family, the shepherds, and other biblical characters were set on rotating platforms within a large pyramid-shaped structure. Heat from candles turned rotors, which made the platforms revolve.

Especially in the Oberammergau region of Germany wood carving has been raised to the level of high art. In the long winters, farmers carve the charming wooden

During the Christmas season the descendants of the Moravians go *Putz* visiting, traveling from house to house to view the neighbors' *Putz*. The women sometimes wear traditional family costumes to receive visitors.

Bethlehem, Pennsylvania, has a large community *Putz* at the First Moravian Church. It includes a stream of running water, 200 buildings (including a scale-model of Herod's temple), and figures hand carved from mahogany.

In other parts of the New World folk artists used available materials to fashion nativity sets. On midwestern farms Christmas cribs were made from the husks, stalks, and tassels of corn. In the mountains of Tennessee and Kentucky crib figures were carved from the roots and stumps of the poplar tree and from horse chestnut or pine wood.

The Spanish and Portuguese who colonized Central and South America introduced the

Materials and artistry may vary, but the focus of the crèche is always the same—the Christ child in the manger! The crèche from Sweden (left) is constructed from very simple materials, straw and wood. The crèche from Oberammergau, Germany, (right) shows masterful craftsmanship. The entire piece is about six inches high. The figures are minute, carved from wood and set within the onion-dome shrine.

nacimiento or *pesebre* there. Today in many parts of Latin America folk artists create simple figures in a primitive art style. In Mexico figures are made from sticks and dressed in bits of cloth. In Guatemala they are modeled from clay and hand fired. In Peru we can find the *retablo,* a small wooden box, brightly painted, in which are placed small figures made from papier-maché or bread dough. In Ecuador rattan is used, and the *nacimiento* is displayed on circular mats.

A favorite pastime in Brazil at Christmas is the making of the *pesebre.* Brightly colored sand is used to form hills and plains. On Christmas Eve the Christ child is placed in the crib. Beginning on Christmas the Wise Men are moved forward a little each day to symbolize their journey from the East to Bethlehem.

At Christmastime children in Puerto Rico flock to the Church of San José at La Navidad, a church so old that Ponce de Lèon worshiped there. There is a large animated *nacimiento,* a complete village with mechanized villagers going about their daily work or traveling the countryside on toy trains.

In Mexico on Candlemas, February 2, candles are burned before the manger in which the Christ child lies. The family appoints two members as honorary godparents of the baby, and they come forward to present the type of small gifts given at the baptism of a Mexican child.

As Christian missionaries carried the gospel to Africa and Asia, the traditions of Christmas accompanied them. Here Third World Christians follow their traditional art forms to create the Christmas crib. In Africa and Madagascar, where the woods of mahogany, ebony, and thistlewood abound, carvers depict biblical characters with African features and wearing local costumes. In India manger figures are made from brass and copper printing blocks. In the Philippines figures are carved from shell and hand painted.

And so from the first Christmas in Bethlehem nearly 2000 years ago, the Christmas crib has circled the globe. In each land where the wondrous story of Christmas has been told, believers have responded by recreating the nativity scene. Today in churches and shopping centers, in villages and cities, in huts and mansions, the presence of the Christmas crib reminds us of the true meaning of Christmas and recalls the words of the angel: "I bring you good news of a great joy which will come to all the people; for to you is born this day in the city of David a Savior who is Christ the Lord. And this will be a sign for you: you will find a babe wrapped in swaddling cloths and lying in a manger."

People around the world recall Jesus' birth with the crèche.

Israel's olive trees provide the material for this beautiful crèche. Each piece in the set is hand carved. Notice the extreme variation of color and grain in the olive wood. A crèche from the land of Jesus' birth!

This crèche, too, is carved from wood, this time from Nigeria. Two kinds of wood are used: light-colored wood for the clothing and headwear, dark-colored wood for the skin. The headwear and clothes are representative of that country's culture; the features are those of its people. This style of wood carving is popular in Nigeria, used to picture all kinds of activities common to that country.

Adoration of the Shepherds

Rembrandt Harmensz van Rijn, 1606-1669

PHILLIP GUGEL

The "Adoration of the Shepherds," painted by Rembrandt in 1646, emphasizes the humble circumstances of Jesus' birth. No angels hover overhead as in Correggio's or Murillo's version of the shepherds' visit. Nor does the event occur outside in a lyrical landscape with many figures and elegant classical architecture, as in Ghirlandajo's version. Rembrandt's night scene takes place in a barn. The unpretentious rural folk pictured probably resemble the inhabitants whom Rembrandt saw during his visits to the Dutch countryside in search of subjects to sketch.

A mysterious light, hidden from view, illumines the central figures around the Christ child. Jesus, Mary, Joseph, a couple with a child, and the kneeling shepherds are bathed in the light's warm, golden radiance. Judging from their gestures, the shepherds are awestruck. Rembrandt has grouped his central figures as if they are gathered around the family hearth. The barn's main post accents their off-center position in the foreground of the painting.

Other shepherds enter from the right, led by an elderly man wearing a broad-brimmed hat and carrying a lantern, the picture's one realistic source of light. But its flame is dim compared to the bright light illumining the central figures. J. Bolten and H. Bolten-Rempt interpret this contrast as an allusion to the fourth evangelist's words: "The true light that enlightens every man was coming into the world" (John 1:9).

A woman nestling her child, and two other persons follow the elderly man. They are illumined by another hidden light source behind them. These figures have not yet sensed the wonder of this occasion. In the distance it is possible to detect two other blurred figures peering in the barn's rear window. Next to the elderly man are a boy and his dog, figures Rembrandt repeats from an earlier version of the "Adoration of the Shepherds," painted in 1641 after his beloved wife Saskia gave birth to their son Titus. During the 1640s, according to Ludwig Münz, Rembrandt repeatedly painted scenes from Jesus' youth. Perhaps in them he was expressing his joy over Titus, the only one of their four children who survived infancy.

Mary's red blouse and bluish-green skirt and the red blouse of the woman to her left are the only bright color areas relieving Rembrandt's monochromatic hues. By using somber colors, indistinct figural outlines, and zones of velvety shadows, he unifies all the figures.

The diagonal and horizontal lines of the barn's beams, loft, and rafters make its interior seem spacious and three-dimensional. Behind the holy family, the ox and ass fade into the middle plane, while above them two birds—perhaps chickens—are perched on the loft. It is not hard to imagine that the pattern of lines made by the barn's central post, its brace, and the ladder leaning against the loft partially forms the monogram "XP," the first two letters of the Greek word for Christ (*XPISTOS*). These two letters form the Latin monogram for peace (*pax*) as well. Though it is unknown if Rembrandt intended this hidden symbolism, it serves as a reminder that Christmas lies in the shadows of Good Friday and Easter.

Some scholars have identified the large, oval-shaped object on the barn's central post as a basket or an empty saddle. In John Milton's poem, "On the Morning of Christ's Nativity" (1629), he mentions a shield "high up-hung," one of several references to ancient weapons (also a chariot and spear) which are put away on the day of Jesus' birth, lauded by Milton as a time of peace. It is unknown if Rembrandt read this poem, but he did include classical elements in some of his pictures. It is likely, then, that this is a shield on the barn's post, a sort of "faceless heathen god" as Sir Kenneth Clark imagines it, which symbolizes the world into which Jesus came, bringing light and peace.

The painting's brushwork has broad, free, painterly qualities which unify its figures and forms. The figures are not sharply delineated, and their faces show a minimum of detailing, an indication Rembrandt was more concerned with the picture's overall unity than with the individual personalities of the holy family and their visitors.

Art historians have not discovered who commissioned Rembrandt to paint the "Adoration of the Shepherds." But another version of this episode, also executed by him in 1646, was completed as the result of a commission from Prince Frederick Henry of Orange. Rembrandt has left three paintings and an etching of the shepherds' visit to the Christ child as part of his artistic legacy.

Unlike most Dutch artists of his time, who were more interested in genre scenes, landscapes, portraits, and still lifes, Rembrandt produced hundreds of drawings, etchings, and paintings of biblical subjects throughout his life. He had a particular interest in the women of the Old Testament and in those episodes which relate to Jesus' humanity. Though he painted many nonbiblical subjects as well, the Bible remained an inexhaustible source of inspiration for Rembrandt's genius.

Rembrandt's biblical pictures are an expression of his deep faith. In the "Adoration of the Shepherds" he left his response to John's words about the mystery of that child whose humble birth united the family of mankind: "And the Word became flesh and dwelt among us, full of grace and truth."

The Season of Gwiazdka

Christmas in Hungary, Poland, and Slovakia*

LA VERN J. RIPPLEY

As in perhaps 50 other countries St. Nicholas Day, December 6, officially opens the Christmas festivities in Poland, Slovakia, and Hungary. We know little about Nicholas, other than that he lived in the late third and early fourth centuries during the reigns of the Roman emperors Diocletian, Maximilian, and Constantine. Consecrated Archbishop of Myra, he died in A.D. 326 on December 6. His influence today, however, stretches to the extremities of Christian civilization, to the Laplanders and fishermen of the Arctic, to the streets and villages of America, but nowhere more completely than in the vast expanses of Eastern Europe.

According to legend, Nicholas' parents died when he was young, leaving him a large fortune. In one instance Nicholas provided bags of gold to young women of marriageable age so that they would have dowries to attract respectable husbands. On another occasion, a nobleman's three sons were traveling to Myra to get Nicholas' blessing when they were overwhelmed in a hostelry and murdered. Made aware of the event in a vision, Nicholas rushed to the scene, apprehended the innkeeper, and raised the boys to life. In these two legends are the seeds of today's Santa Claus of the West and of the widely celebrated Feast of St. Nicholas in Eastern Europe.

For centuries the heritage of St. Nicholas grew. In the Middle Ages children dressed a boy as Nicholas and were themselves his retinue. Together they roamed the streets collecting tribute from burghers during the period from December 6 until the feast of the Holy Innocents on December 28, the day commemorating King Herod's slaughter of Judean children.

Much of the Nicholas pageantry has faded in Eastern Europe, but in Poland, Slovakia, and Hungary St. Nicholas still appears in robes and miter, sometimes riding a white steed and wearing a scarlet jacket with white fleece trimmings.

In Polish rural mountain villages he is called Mikolaja; he is dressed in a long white robe and rides a sleigh pulled by spirited horses. Everywhere his duty is the same: to rebuke the mischievous, praise the obedient, and pass out gifts. Frequently these consist of food, almost always including big red apples and heart-shaped honey cookies called *pierniki* in Poland.

In Slovakia St. Mikulase (Nicholas) is said to descend from heaven on a golden cord, his back laden with a basket full of apples, nuts, and candy. As in Poland, the Slovakian Nicholas is accompanied by a mentor who is dressed in black and carries switches to punish naughty boys and girls, in particular those who cannot say their prayers when Nicholas asks for a rendition. If necessary, he leaves a switch behind to be used by the parents. Wherever children are already asleep, St. Nicholas leaves toys and candy in the shoes of the good, potato or onion peelings in those of the wicked.

In Hungary St. Nicholas visits every home where children live, if not in person, then by filling shoes left on window sills with goodies or with a piece of coal or a switch—as the case may require. In regions of Hungary where the Austrian influence was strong, notably in the southern part, Nicholas takes the form of a fur-wearing, unchurchly figure and bears the name Pleznickel ("fur-skin Nicholas"). Pleznickel grew out of several pagan Alpine characters who used animal masks to admonish errant boys and girls. As a fur-fitted figure, this Nicholas fulfilled both roles, that of the saint and that of his black-robed mentor, known as Knecht Ruprecht in the Germanic tradition.

Although each country provides its own variation, the St. Nicholas tradition is a common theme which links these areas in Eastern Europe. In many ways the celebration of the great feast of Christmas is quite similar throughout Poland, Slovakia, and Hungary, and this is not due to sheer coincidence. The entire Eastern European region has a historical unity because the Christian net was cast across the area uniformly.

As descendants of Finno-Ugric tribes who migrated to the region from the Ural Mountains of Russia, Hungarians built on the culture of earlier peoples in their land—the Celts, the Romans, the Huns, and various Slavic tribes. By the 11th century Hungary was established as an independent Christian kingdom headed by Stephen (1001-1038) who was canonized St. Stephen for his success in Christianizing his people. A large kingdom in the 14th century, Hungary once included most of present-day Romania, the states of northern Yugoslavia, all of Slovakia, and portions of eastern Poland. After 1500, Hungary fell victim to competing superior forces—the Holy Roman emperors (usually the Hapsburgs) to the west and the Ottoman Empire of the Turks to the southeast. With the defeat of the Turks at Vienna in 1683, Hungary fell under the Hapsburg dynasty, which lasted with periodic modifications until 1918. Under Maria Theresa (1717-1780) Germanic culture was imposed, the aristocracy was absorbed into her empire, and the population and its traditions were diffused by the importation of colonists from Germany.

---

*Slovakia is the eastern half of present-day Czechoslovakia. Once a separate country, it was merged with Bohemia and Moravia in 1918 to form the country of Czechoslovakia. Slovakia has its own language and culture, quite distinct from the rest of the country. The Slovakian district forms a geographical belt, north to south, with Poland and Hungary. See the map on page 26.

Poland received Christianity at almost the same time as greater Hungary. Integrated into the West in the 10th century, Poland's first recorded king was Mieszko who pledged allegiance to the Holy Roman emperor in Germany, became a Christian, and in 966 acknowledged the papacy. For a few centuries (1386-1572) under the Jagiellon dynasty, Poland's borders extended beyond Lithuania and included most of Czechoslovakia and Hungary. But weakened by internal strife and religious conflict, by 1650 Poland had been invaded by Russia, deprived of Prussia by the Germans, and pressured by Swedish potentates. In 1772, in 1791, and finally in 1793, an enfeebled Poland fell victim to partition by Germany, Austria, and Russia. The Polish nation had ceased to exist, but the traditions lived on. Throughout the 19th century the occupiers waged an intensive campaign to eradicate Polish culture. Then World War 1 erupted, and both sides of the conflict tried to enlist the support of the Poles by promising them unification. The promise of unification was realized with the Treaty of Versailles in 1919.

Today Poland is almost entirely Roman Catholic with minorities of Lutherans, Polish Orthodox, and some Jews. In the whole of Czechoslovakia—created out of Bohemia, Moravia, and Slovakia in 1918—Roman Catholics are in the majority. Although no official statistics are kept, it is well known that Slovakia has a large Lutheran element in its population of four million. Czechoslovakia historically had been a haven for religious dissidents in Western Europe and to this day includes a Hungarian minority and Polish national Ukrainian church members interspersed among the Roman Catholics. Hungary is about 60% Catholic, with a 20% minority of Reformed Swiss Calvinists, about 6% Lutherans, and a host of other groups.

Creche scenes and nativity plays, part of this Roman Catholic tradition, are an integral part of Eastern Europe's Christmas festivities. The most elaborate and most highly developed Christmas crèche collections are in Poland, some of the finest being in the ethnic museum of Krakow in southern Poland. Elaborate wooden and cardboard models are intricately crafted and painstakingly decorated in the best traditions of Polish folk art. They have an elegance fit for the newborn King but are scarcely representative of the humble stable. The crèche scene in these lands usually stays in place from Christmas Day to Candlemas Day on February 2 and depicts not only the shepherds and the three kings, but other biblical stories—such as Herod's soldiers slaying infants, the flight into Egypt, and especially the wedding feast at Cana. Over the years the scene has grown constantly, until it incorporates many everyday characters—nobles, peasants, farmers with their wagons of grain, women milking cows, bakers making bread, and Jewish merchants selling wares.

In Poland *kolednicy* (carolers) carry a lighted, multicolored star illuminated from the inside with a candle or lantern (possibly a flashlight) and stream through the neighborhoods singing the merry *koledy*. In addition to the illuminated star, a portable nativity set is frequently borne by the troupe, many of whom have dressed themselves as shepherds, King Herod, soldiers, the devil, Jewish merchants, or even the Grim Reaper (death).

In the Hungarian and Slovakian regions traveling nativity puppets include such figures as the peddler, the medicine man, the Hungarian hussar, the gypsy with a bear, and other rural folk characters. Costumes and head dress vary from village to village but usually include uniforms, church vestments, and royal garments. Children (known as *Betlehemci*) also travel the streets of villages, performing nativity plays. They either carry crèche sets or play the parts of the holy family, the shepherds, and the magi.

These activities reach a high point on St. Lucia's Day, December 13. On this important festival the Hungarian young men embellish the plays with ancient rituals of light. In former times, a fire was ignited outside every home in the village, and villagers moved from one home to the next chanting traditional verses that asked for the health and fertility of their domestic animals and families.

In America we think of St. Lucia's Day on December 13 as a Swedish Christmas festival. In reality St. Lucia's Day also belongs to the folkloric celebration of Christmas in central Europe. Lucia is a legendary figure from the nebulous early centuries of Christianity. Her name (from the Latin *lux, lucis*) suggests light, and her feast day coincides with the ancient calculations of the shortest day of the year. In Sweden and in Sicily, St. Lucia commemorates the rebirth of light both by her name and by her ethos—allegedly she had her eyes plucked out when a prince found them so beautiful that he tried to ravish her in a convent.

St. Lucia's Day is not celebrated in Poland, but Advent does call for the preparation of another light symbol— a star. In Poland the star is used more than any other ornament. Christmas itself is known by that name— *Gwiazdka* or "little star." Consequently starlets predominate over all other decorations used during the season. In the oldest tradition the stars were made of straw or of duck and goose feathers (the traditional fowl of Polish villages) glued together with candle wax. Later, beautiful models were created out of wood chips and shavings. Today larger stars made by the best local talent embellish the altar and sanctuary of the village church, and every Polish Christmas tree has many artistic stars cut from colorful, intricately folded construction paper.

The Christmas tree, or *choinka*, is a spruce if possible and, in all three countries, is seldom decorated before Christmas Eve. If it must be decorated earlier, then it is hidden away in a spare room and brought forth during the festivities of the holy evening. Decorations for the tree are made beforehand in the form of stars and mobiles, some of which are hung from a chandelier or the ceiling. The tree is decorated exclusively with homemade crafts: straw stars ranking highest, paper stars, fruits, nuts, and baked honey cookies. Intricately decorated egg shells also belong on the Christmas tree and not just in the Easter basket. The egg symbolizes the miracle of birth and, in Poland especially, duck and goose eggs are decorated with rich, geometric designs and hung on the tree. Often the craftsperson adds a base and spout to form a pitcher or urn. Sometimes the eggs are painted with the face of a Polish historical person, an angel, or a figure from the crèche.

Slovakia

The most solemn moments of the Polish Christmas season come during the celebration of the *Wilia* (the family-oriented Christmas Eve event with its traditional supper) and the *Pasterka* (literally the "shepherd's mass" held at midnight in the local church). In many ways, the *Wilia* (or *Wigilia*) on December 24 is the most sacred, solemn, symbolic, and nostalgic day of the year. Acknowledged for centuries (however inaccurately) as the longest night of the year, the eve of Christmas symbolizes the retriumph of light over darkness. Traditionally the Poles ate little all day on the 24th. In part, this was necessary because everyone was busy preparing for the big evening meal, in part because until recently Catholics fasted on the day before Christmas.

Shoppers find a plentiful supply of fish at the market when they come to buy for the evening meal. Until recently, December 24 was a meatless day by church law. All day long, adults bake; children help clean, grind poppy seed, and bring in wood for the fires. Animals are provided with an extra supply of fodder. The best sheaves of last year's harvest of grain are arrayed in corners of the living room. Sweet-smelling hay and perhaps some spears of wheat and rye are scattered on the *Wilia* table beneath the fresh linen tablecloth. Associated in pagan times with the rebirth of nature, these traditions now remind Eastern Europeans of the birth of Jesus in a manger.

Excluded from the Polish *Wilia* supper are foods that require the meat or fat of animals, which are to be treated like humans on this day. Nuts, honey, berries, grains, cereals, vegetables, fruit, and of course fish are the standard fare, delicately baked and prepared. Some families serve up to a dozen different kinds of fish, the most traditional being *karp* and herring. With everything in readiness, the children begin their vigil watching for the first star. The first star to shine in the heavens symbolizes the triumph of light over darkness. When it makes its appearance, the oldest child or perhaps the father of the family cries out and everyone knows the sacred moment has arrived. In Slovakian villages, children watch for either a star or a radiant angel to appear in the heavens. Some families light the candles on the Christmas tree and enjoy its natural lights for a few moments before dining. Others gather immediately at the *Wilia* table where one chair and place setting are left empty for the invisible Holy Guest.

Before the feasting begins, the ancient rite of the *oplatek* (in Slovakia, the *oplatki*) is reenacted. Taken from the Latin word *oblatum* meaning "an offering" (and by extension to the Catholic mass, "the sacred bread") the *oplatek* is a wafer of choice wheat grains made since the 10th century arrival of Christianity in Poland. Always white, the liturgical wafer usually is made with iron plates on which a craftsperson has engraved various motifs: the stable in Bethlehem, the holy family, perhaps a scene of geese or sheep on a farm, the three kings, a church, or familiar birds in a tree. Sometimes the thin wafer is suspended over the *Wilia* table where it twists and sways with a touch of spirit as the guests express their wishes and prayers. Occasionally the wafers are cut into star shapes and added to the Christmas tree.

The most intimate moment of the Christmas season arrives when the hostess or head of the house takes the frail *oplatek*, pronounces the words of love and sharing, and then breaks and distributes the wafer to all present. In Slovakia, altar boys bear *oplatki* wrapped in embroidered cloth to the homes of all the needy and the sick. Across the nation and throughout the world, scattered members of extended families all feel united as one through this symbolic staff of life, this bread of blessing, this communal act of forgiveness and family warmth. Today in the United States, *oplatek* wafers are available from specialty bakeries, especially in Polish-American communities.

Following the supper, concluded by *piernik* (ginger cake), fruit compote of pears, peaches, apples, or plums, poppy-seed cake, candies and nuts, guests often drink a glass of *krupnik*, a holiday brandy made of honey and oriental spices. In Slovakia it's *slivovica*, in Hungary it's *slivowitz*. Thereafter the hostess gathers up the table linens and shakes them outside for the birds and chickens. Importantly, the remains of the *oplatek* are mixed with fodder for the cattle and other domestic animals that warmed the babe in Bethlehem. Again the Christmas tree is lighted. Girls sometimes pull a spear of hay from the table to foretell what kind of man they will marry, and all join in for carols. The greatest gift of the evening is not in the form of presents under the tree but of fellowship in the intimacy of one's family. Santa Claus does not exist in Eastern Europe, but a version of St. Nicholas sometimes comes in the form of a star man dressed in a bear skin with a hood of lamb's wool, wearing a white beard, who passes from house to house. Otherwise, it is the Christ child who brings the gifts.

Pasterka, the shepherd's mass at midnight, draws the entire Polish community together. Bells ring, lights in cottages blink out, people stream in to celebrate *Gwiazdka* ("the little star"—Christmas). In former times, young men carried a lighted star on a pole or wore it on their heads when they went to *pasterka*. Inside, talented organists imitate the sounds of birds and animals that were present at Jesus' birth. Interspersed throughout the service are many *kolendy*, religious carols that sprang from local composers. In Slovakia and Hungary too the fish supper is followed by midnight mass in a traditional Catholic church.

Throughout much of Europe, Christmas Day is celebrated not just on December 25, but on the 26th as well. The first of these two days is reserved for rather close family members, the second for visiting throughout the community and more distant relatives. For December 25 there is also a traditional menu with meat as the main feature. Dating from pagan times, pork has been the popular choice with ham the ultimate specialty. A variety of sausages together with mushrooms is always available. Also popular is *bigos* or hunter's stew—a mixture of several meats, wild if available, cooked outdoors in large kettles with vegetables and sauerkraut. There is plenty of rye bread, strudel, and good pastries—many made with poppy seeds—to satisfy even the hungriest traveler.

December 26 is St. Stephen's Day, celebrated especially in Hungary and Slovakia where the saint is of special significance. Because weddings and baptisms are not performed during Advent, St. Stephen's Day is sometimes used to catch up on these necessities. People take gifts to their clergymen, hitch teams to sleighs, and gallavant about, visiting friends and relatives at longer distances. Polish carolers again make their rounds and in public places villagers witness the *jaselka* or *szopki,* the manger scene. Fiddles come out of their cases, and people dance together. *Gwiazdore,* or star bearers, appear in the streets; each young lad carries a pole on which is mounted a paper star with a lighted candle encased in the center. By pulling a string, the star spins rapidly. Some troupes sing carols, others perform nativity plays or put on puppet shows about the nativity. Sometimes the characters are costumed, dressed as a buffalo or a goat, perhaps, or wearing a symbolic wooden mask, maybe a wolf or a bear. Occasionally these creatures, undoubtedly of pagan origin, run at women and young girls to frighten them.

In this area, New Year's Eve is known as St. Sylvester's Day. On this day the Hungarians indulge their love of roast pig, partly because well-seasoned roast pork is a favorite, partly because the pig in many European folk traditions is a good luck symbol. There are, of course, many parties and dancing; then at the stroke of midnight, firecrackers, whip cracking, and shooting fill the night air. An old Polish Sylvester tradition calls for young girls to dash from house to house picking up some article belonging to a young man. That evening youthful villagers gather to auction off their loot, usually to the owner, which garners enough money for a festive party. Some families bake special cakes and cookies sculptured like the animals of the forest or with scenes of village life. In some families, the Sylvester supper is almost as important as the *Wilia* of Christmas Eve. New Year's Day is usually spent feasting with family and friends.

The last major event in the Christmas season is Epiphany on January 6. Following church services, the parish priest tours the village to bless homes by marking on the door with blessed chalk the initials of the magi: *K* for Kaspar, *M* for Melchior, and *B* for Balthazar. He places a small cross between each letter. If the priest cannot reach all homes, people bring chalk to be blessed and mark the *K M B* themselves as a means of insuring protection for the home during the following year. In Slovakia peasants receive water and incense blessed in the church. They sprinkle their homes and burn the incense to insure protection of their families and farmlands.

In Eastern Europe the Christmas season dies down after Epiphany, revives momentarily at Candlemas, but is not finally extinguished until Ash Wednesday. In Poland this is the period for a big winter sleigh party, or *kulig.* Depending on the geographic region, this celebration might last several days. Families congregate, people visit neighbors, the hosts load their tables with foods. In certain communities, *kulig* has the carnival atmosphere of pre-Lenten hilarity. In others it combines with a birthday or name day or anniversary. Merrymakers set off firecrackers, traditional costumes are worn, bells ring out, and merriment is boundless. There is dancing, much feasting, and ample supplies of cake and wine.

Today some of the intimate traditions of Eastern Europe seem to lie dormant. The state frowns on religious practice, yet in a few schizophrenic situations will provide financial support for religious observances. In this unfriendly atmosphere on October 16, 1978, Karol Wojtyla of Krakow, Poland, was elected Pope John Paul II. Not since the Dutch pope, Adrian VI (1522-1523) had a non-Italian been named to that position. Having earned doctorates in both theology and ethics, Wojtyla first lectured at the Jagiellonian University in Krakow and later was named bishop and cardinal of that diocese. A powerful leader in the Polish church's stand for Christian rights, John Paul II brought new hope and renewed optimism for the Christians of Eastern Europe.

Hope and optimism—of these the Christmas season is legendary.

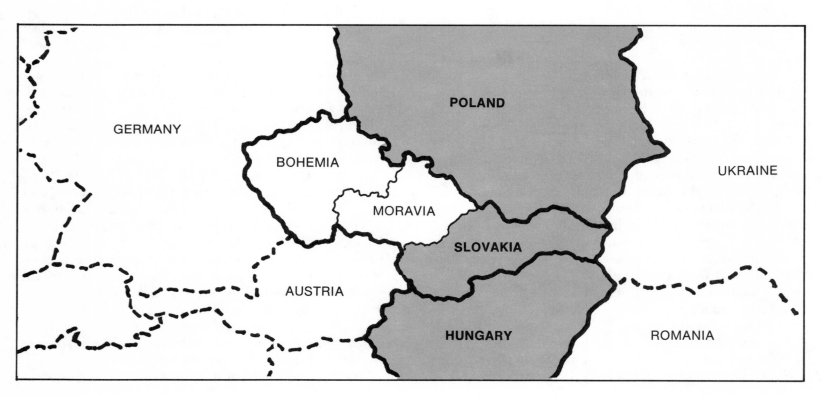

The Gifts They Gave

WILSON C. EGBERT

Jesus was born in Israel, a land occupied by a foreign army, seething with unrest and change; it was a crossroads of dissimilar cultures, languages, and life-styles. When some magi appeared in Jerusalem asking about "the newborn king," a suspicious monarch set out to destroy this threat to his shaky power. Before he was two years old, Jesus fled the country as part of a refugee family.

Nor has Christmas always been a quiet, peaceable celebration in the centuries following Christ's birth. Great souls have observed Christmas in times of danger and stress. We will meet a few of them. What they went through, what they did and said, and what they were became the fabric of the gifts they gave to their Lord and, in many instances, to those around them.

David Livingstone

In the 19th century the name of David Livingstone was the topic of many a conversation and newspaper article. A missionary, explorer, medicine man, and linguist, Livingstone was captivated by the continent of Africa. During his first term in Africa Livingstone established a mission station despite opposition from the slave-trading Boers who occupied the area. Slavers grew to hate him because he used his influence to stop their trade

in human beings. Livingstone also was mauled by a lion in those early years, which left him with a crippled arm for the rest of his life.

Besides mission work Livingstone set out to explore the uncharted areas of interior Africa, hoping to open it to Western civilization. He mapped rivers, settlements, towns, and lakes. He gave form to the study of African languages, which were totally unlike the Roman and Greek grammatical forms scholars had been using. As a naturalist he made records of animal, insect, and plant life and sent specimens back to British museums and scientists. But most of all, wherever he went he preached the gospel of Jesus Christ.

His wife, Mary Moffat, accompanied him on these journeys until she could no longer keep pace with him. Malaria, ague, dysentery, and sleeping sickness stalked the country they crossed. Thieves stole medicines, food, and supplies. Finally, it was decided that Mary should take their children to be raised and educated in the safer climate of the British Isles. After Christmas in 1848, Livingstone wrote to his father-in-law, Robert Moffat:

> Most of our boxes which come to us from England are opened and usually lightened of their contents. You will probably remember one. . . . It contained, on leaving Glasgow, a parcel of surgical instruments which I ordered and of course paid for. . . . The box which you kindly packed for us and dispatched to Glasgow has, we hear, been gutted by Custom House thieves.

Turning his explorations to search for the sources of Africa's great rivers, Livingstone wrestled with the ache of separation from his family as well as advancing age and poor health. On Christmas Day 1869, he wrote:

> December 25. We start immediately after Christmas. I must try with all my might to finish my exploration before next Christmas.

Only three Christmases remained for this 20th century Wise Man. He would die in his beloved Africa surrounded by the people to whom he had devoted so much of his life. His last Christmas Day journal entry strikes the constant theme of his life:

> I thank the good Lord for the good gift of His Son Jesus Christ our Lord. Slaughtered an ox and gave a fundo and a half to each of the party. This is our great day, so we rest. It is cold and wet, day and night. The headsman is gracious and generous.

Hans Engede

A little more than a century earlier, another missionary, linguist, and sometime explorer braved the cold wilderness of Greenland. His commitment to preach the gospel among the Eskimo people in this rugged land was first stirred by stories of early Viking settlements there.

To learn the language and needs of the Greenlanders,

David Livingstone

Hans Egede spent hours in the stench-filled huts of the Inuit. More than once he was confronted by the sullen anger and the shrieking incantations of their medicine men, the *Angakoks*. Finally, at Christmastime 1723, Egede and an assistant completed a catechism in the language of the people.

Twelve years passed. Sickness ravaged the area. The ministry to the Inuit and the training of new missionaries sapped Egede's physical strength. Then on Christmas Day 1735, Egede wrote in his diary:

> It has pleased Almighty God to take from me my beloved wife. If it were not for the comforting hope of a reunion in the Kingdom of Glory, I would scarcely be able to console myself in the face of the loss of such a spiritual and faithful helpmate. As a child of God she bore the cross which was laid upon her with great patience. . . . God delivered her from her severe sufferings through a blessed death.

By 1736, Hans Egede had to leave Greenland because of exhaustion. Behind him he left Christian Inuit, two young missionaries, three native catechists, and his son Poul, "the maker of words who could teach them of the Lord God." To the Greenlanders he left a grammar and word book, translated portions of the gospels, and a simple catechism. These were his Christmas gifts to the Lord.

Henry Melchior Muhlenberg

At about the same time Hans Egede was training missionaries to take his place in Greenland, a young German pastor set sail from England to minister in America. In 1742, Spanish privateers threatened the seas, so his ship, the *Georgia Packet*, delayed leaving England for three weeks in the hope of better winds and a naval escort. Finally the ship left the safety of English waters and guns. Water was foul, and the daily fare of peas, pork, stockfish, and salt beef "half-cooked in the English manner" did not make the trip a pleasure. Quarrelsome and drunken sailors, the profanity of the crew and his English cabinmates, and rats "so numerous one could count several thousands" did not allay Henry Melchior Muhlenberg's persistent seasickness. Land's End to Charleston was a 75-day misery.

From Charleston to Philadelphia the way was no easier. To ride overland would take Muhlenberg through swamps and along mud "traces" that served as roads. To go by sea ran the risk of Spanish seizure of ship and crew. Over either way loomed the stormy weather of November and December. Muhlenberg looked at his flattening purse and took passage on a Philadelphia bound sloop. Nine days of a November storm brought them to a Delaware haven. The cabin held three passengers. Since the crew could not sleep on deck, they crowded in as well. Finally, 13 days enroute, the new pastor of Providence and New Hannover landed in Philadelphia.

The weather still tested Muhlenberg. A heavy rain and high water made roads almost impassable, yet he had promised to hold a confessional service at New Hannover:

> December 24, Friday. They gave me a strong horse with which I was able to plunge through and reach New Hannover. Arrived about two o'clock, but had to remain there because the water rose so high that we were unable to reach the church.
>
> December 25, Christmas Day. The waters had receded again, so we were able to get to church. In spite of the terrible roads there was a large gathering present, and we held divine service.

In the years that followed, Muhlenberg busied himself ministering not only to his parish but also to congregations scattered from Culpepper, Virginia, to East Camp on the upper Hudson River.

By 1775, the Colonies were seething with revolt. The prospect of war with new floods of displaced people was on Muhlenberg's mind as he considered buying a small property to serve as his parsonage. At Christmas he wrote:

> On the strength of available news and in the light of all appearances, it seems the flames of war will spread farther over the united North American provinces during the coming year, unless the Lord God, the Supreme Ruler, determines otherwise.
>
> In consideration of its nearness to one of our original congregations, . . . and because a place (neither too near the city nor too near the Indian frontier) is needed in the present crisis as a refuge for fleeing pastors, their families, widows, etc., I resolved to buy the place.

Henry Melchior Muhlenberg

By Christmas 1776, the mood was sober indeed. The American armies had suffered stinging defeats. Washington's brigades were camped on the Delaware River opposite Trenton, New Jersey. There were stories of atrocities and of a possible attack on Philadelphia by the British navy. Christmas Day's entry was solemn:

> December 25, Wednesday. We celebrated the festival of Christmas. I preached on the festival Gospel in Augustus Church and announced that service would be held, God willing, on the Sunday after New Year. . . .

On that night the victory at Trenton took place and for a moment the tide of battle turned. But a year later the British held Philadelphia, and British cavalry scoured the countryside at will. On Christmas Eve 1777, the aging pastor wrote: "I am receiving one report after another that the British officers are extremely angry at me and are seeking to apprehend me."

December 25, Thursday, Christmas Day. The weather was bitter cold. In the forenoon went to church and held divine service with the congregation. I mentioned among other things that last year about this time the chastening and punishing hand of God had been at Trenton, only 30 miles away. . . .

It is becoming more and more dangerous from day to day in our own region of Providence. . . . Our friends are earnestly advising that we two old folks should flee to Tulpehaken; but we cannot, for winter is here, the road is bad, transportation is too scarce, and victuals are dear everywhere; and besides, we old folks are too feeble for a journey in winter.

Five more Christmases were to pass before the peace treaty was signed. A new nation was being established and Muhlenberg continued to offer the only Christmas gift he had left—faithfulness to God's people under fire.

Clara Maass

Daniel Nelson

In 1882 a Norwegian sailor set in motion a chain of events that paused only briefly at his death in the cross-fire of battle at Sinyang, China, on February 8, 1926. A veteran of four shipwrecks in his 10 years at sea, he had once been rescued by a Chinese fishing crew.

When his call came to go to China as a missionary, Daniel Nelson was shingling the roof of the third house he had built for his family in America. He had an 80-acre farm with livestock and machinery. By that time Nelson's

family numbered four children, with another expected. His wife, Anna, questioned Nelson's decision to go to China but finally gave her consent. The sale of most of their possessions brought enough money to pay for transportation and the shipping of a few necessary household goods. At that point the family had $500 left. Friends would need to take up the slack because, the mission board reasoned, Nelson was 37 years old, had a family, and was "only" an untrained layman.

The Nelson family spent their first Christmas in China at Wuchang, across the river from Hankow. They lived in a small three-room adobe house. Three small houses were crowded on a lot measuring 50 by 100 feet and surrounded by a 10-foot wall. Outside was a mud court-yard, inside was a mud floor.

Four years later, Christmas Day 1894, Daniel Nelson baptized two Chinese converts in Hankow. He had been busy in many areas: securing a site for a mission in Fancheng and directing the activities of other missionaries in Honan and Hupeh provinces. Then during the summer of 1891, the family had to flee to Wuchang after two Swedish missionaries had been brutally murdered in the area. Cries of "Kill the foreign devils" were beginning to be heard. This slogan marked the years till the Boxer Rebellion in 1900, which took hundreds of lives. The Nelson family was on sick leave and furlough in the United States at the time and thus was spared.

When Nelson returned to China, he took building materials and his family on an open railroad flatcar toward Sinyang. Where the tracks ran out, coolies were hired to carry in the cargo. Nelson now acted as architect and builder and missionary. On Christmas Day 1902, he baptized 11 adults and 2 children. Christian faith had taken root in Sinyang.

Over the years Nelson exhibited many gifts. He became a skilled planner and administrator, a financier and diplomat, a musician, poet, and writer. When Christmas 1925 rolled around, China was torn by civil war. The Christian general, Feng-yu-hsiang, had left a small garrison to protect Sinyang. Christian schools, a hospital, and mission stations were clustered at each of the four principal city gates.

The southern army under Wu-pei-fu seized the railroad and began moving north from Hankow.

On Christmas Day the church was packed, and Nelson took his place in the pulpit. Political unrest had not kept people from attending church, but brought more people in, as if in a search for security they had been led into God's presence. It was a great opportunity for Nelson to tell them about God's love and give assurance to those whose faith was weakening. Propaganda students had planned to disrupt the services but when they arrived and saw the church packed with law-abiding people singing joyful songs, they lost their courage.

On January 26, Nelson wrote:

The war that has threatened us so long has finally arrived. No transportation. . . . The air is so full of bullets that it is not safe to go outside.

The south side of the house is exposed to fire through the many windows and doors. . . . We are therefore living in the north side of the house facing the court-yard. Thank the Lord none of us has been hit yet.

On December 31 the fighting was at their door:

There are thousands of refugees crowded into the courtyard, schools, and chapels. . . . Sanitary conditions are a hazard, and difficulty in feeding these refugees worries us. Committees of Christian workers manage to sneak out on the streets and buy rice gruel that is doled out to the most needy. How long we can keep this up is doubtful.

There was no Egypt to which these people could flee. On Sunday, February 7, Nelson had a pulpit placed in the crowded courtyard. The compound was now crowded to standing room only. Under enemy fire he spoke about preparation to meet the Lord. The next evening Nelson was killed. In a lifetime of 73 years, he had spent almost half those years in the service of God in China. The Wise Men had brought rare gifts to the Christ child. So had Daniel Nelson.

Wilfred Grenfell

A ship's surgeon for the Mission to Deep Sea Fishermen sailed up the coasts of Labrador on the fishing smack *Albert*. In the villages where they put in, Wilfred Grenfell found poverty more desperate and grinding than in even the toughest London slums. Men filled their boats every four hours during the best part of the season. Their families cleaned, salted, and dried the catch. But the prices were set so that, at the end of four or five months, the fishermen were still in debt. When Grenfell protested to the merchants and traders, they angrily dismissed him. They preferred things the way they were.

Grenfell sent a blistering letter home:

How could any human being with a heart of flesh, after seeing such sights, enjoy a Christmas dinner in old England, as we hope to, with our minds haunted by these hungry, pale faces. . . . Pray God this voyage of the *Albert* will be repeated again and again.

Grenfell put his life where his words were. By ship in summer and dogsled in winter he acted as physician to the people of Labrador. A biographer, J. Lennox Kerr, described one of the first Christmases Grenfell spent in this bleak land:

When Christmas came he had a large tree erected and decorated, a treat the St. Anthony children had never seen before. Sports were held on the ice on Christmas Day. . . . There were prizes and presents for every child, and the day ended with a concert.

Grenfell started cooperatives that broke the fishermen's bondage to the traders. By hospital and hospital ship he brought medical care where it was needed. His was the gift of healing to the poorest of poor, for the sake of the love of the Lord.

Clara Maass

To the south, at Las Animas Hospital in Havana, Cuba, another medical drama was taking place. A research team was trying to isolate the way yellow fever was communicated. Earlier in the year 1900 two doctors had allowed a mosquito, suspected of being a carrier of the dreaded disease, to bite them. Dr. James Carroll recovered; Dr. Jesse Lazear died. In December a group of three volunteers entered a special building. On December 21 and 22, John J. Moran offered his body to 15 bites from as many suspected carrier mosquitos. On Christmas Day at 11:00

A.M., Moran came down with the fever. He was moved to the hospital for care and recovered. His was a Christmas present to millions of people.

But research wasn't done. Could a vaccine be developed to fight the disease? A nurse on the team kept insisting that she could take part in these dangerous experiments, too. Her first exposure to carrier mosquitos took place on June 4, 1901. She recovered in a week from a light attack. On August 14, she insisted on taking part in another exposure. Some days later she wrote:

Goodby Mother. Don't worry. God will care for me in the yellow fever hospital the same as if I were at home. I will send you nearly all I earn, so be good to yourself and the two little ones. You know I am the man of the family now, but do pray for me.

Clara Maass died on August 24—an early Christmas gift from a nurse dedicated to relieve suffering.

Toyohiko Kagawa

Toyohiko Kagawa of Japan knew suffering at first hand. When he became a Christian in his teens his family

Dietrich Bonhoeffer

and friends disowned him. Soon after he entered seminary training, tuberculosis struck him down. To the word of his doctor that there was no hope, he matched a life of prayer. He had dedicated his life to preach the gospel of Christ. He was certain that God had work for him to do.

A friend told this story:

On Christmas Eve in 1909 he piled all his belongings in a rented cart, and pulling it himself moved into his new home in Shinkawa, the famous slum district of

30

Kobe. His room was a part of a long row of rooms, each of which housed a family. . . . On Christmas Day he heard a loud voice calling at the door, *"Gomen nasai, gomen nasai"* ("please excuse me," a greeting one uses when one calls upon a home). When he went to the door he found a man with a loathesome skin disease. The man said to him, "Who are you?" He answered, "I am Toyohiko Kagawa." The man said, "What are you doing here?" Kagawa replied, "I have come to live here." The visitor said, "This is much too big for one person. I'll come and live with you."

For a moment Kagawa almost said no. Then he remembered that he had come to the Kobe slum to witness to the love of Christ. So he invited the stranger in. Prophet and poet, pastor and social activist, Kagawa made two moves on that Christmas that set a new course for his life.

Dietrich Bonhoeffer

Dietrich Bonhoeffer became a symbol of resistance to oppression—the oppression of Nazi Germany—even from a prison cell. Of the final Christmas before his execution

Dag Hammarskjöld

at Flossenbürg on April 9, 1945, there remain two revealing items. One is a letter to his mother, dated December 28, 1944.

> I am so glad to have just got permission to write you a birthday letter. . . . Dear Mother, I want you to know that I am constantly thinking of you and Father every day, and that I thank God for all that you are to me and the whole family. I know that you have always lived for us and have not lived a life of your own. . . . Thank you for all the love that has come to me in my

cell from you during the past year, and has made every day easier for me. I think these hard years have brought us closer together.

The second item concerns a Christmas package. Bonhoeffer's parents managed to get a Christmas package to him. It, like the treasure of Christian faith and hope, was shared with fellow prisoners.

Eivind Josef Berggrav

To the north another bold Christian proved to be a thorn in the fists of Quisling and Hitler. Bishop Berggrav of Oslo, Norway, managed to survive. Arrested on Good Friday 1942 for his leadership in the Norwegian resistance, he was imprisoned until the liberation of Norway in 1945. In 1958 he sent a last greeting to the first congregation he had served:

> We are getting old, many of us now. I was 74 this fall, and now I would be eligible for the parties for the old folks at Hurdal, as we had them in my time. But every Christmas I feel somehow younger, almost like a child. The difference comes from the fact that eternity is so much closer now. The busyness is over, the quiet is growing. . . .
>
> And so I am sitting in my deep chair, not knowing whether this is my last Christmas. There is nothing sad about the thought. An old man with a life full of weeds and wounds—unbelievable as it sounds—has imputed to him, by God, that which his Redeemer has done for him, and is graciously accepted as a child of God. That is what Christmas is—that God came to earth and took upon himself the condition of men so that we may attain to his. . . . This is not to be fathomed. But it is to be *believed*.

Dag Hammarskjöld

As secretary-general of the United Nations, Dag Hammarskjöld was on his way to negotiate a ceasefire in the Belgian Congo when his plane crashed in Zambia (then Northern Rhodesia), and he was killed. He left behind a devotional notebook, a record of his spiritual wrestling with the reality of Christian revelation and its implication for his life. This book, *Markings*, is considered a classic of religious devotion.

In an entry for Christmas Eve 1960, Dag Hammarskjöld observed: "How proper it is that Christmas should follow Advent. For him who looks toward the future, the manger is situated on Golgotha, and the cross has already been raised in Bethlehem."

Kathryn Koob

Little did another diplomat suspect what lay ahead for her when she accepted an assignment to Iran with the U. S. State Department. Kathryn Koob arrived in Iran in July 1979 to serve as director of the Iran-American Society. On November 4, 1979, angry students stormed the American Embassy, taking captive all Americans there. Koob was a mile away at her office when reports of the takeover arrived. Choosing not to flee, she remained at her post relaying vital information to Washington, D. C. Five hours later, the students surrounded the building, taking Koob hostage as well.

The next day Kathryn was assigned to a tiny bedroom

on the embassy compound. The view from the single window in her bedroom showed the treetops, the sky, and the embassy's communications antenna. The antenna's braces formed a perfect cross and served to remind Kathryn of her Christian faith as the days passed. Hymns and Bible verses learned as a child surfaced to comfort and reassure her. Buoyed by her memories, Kathryn spent the weeks of Advent preparing for Christmas.

Completely shut off from friends and family back home, Kathryn found some comfort in knowing what they would be doing—lighting Advent wreaths, shopping, baking, and planning to get together for the holidays. In lieu of Christmas greetings, she made a special "Christmas card prayer list" and prayed her way thoughtfully through it. "It was amazing how that list kept expanding and how many people it was possible to remember and bless with a prayer."

> The dominant thought that first year was Christmas would be Christmas even if there were no gifts, no tree, no cards, and no family. I remember thinking about these things and saying to myself, "You've always said it. Is it true?" As I moved through the days toward Christmas, I realized finally that indeed it was true.

> Advent worship was a time of reflection on the coming of the Savior. I remember thinking how lucky I was that as a child I had memorized the first 20 verses of Luke 2 so I could have the Christmas story on Christmas Eve. I did not know that I would be given a Bible that evening.

> Christmas Eve, while it brought a Christmas tree from the students and the precious gift of a Bible, was still centered in my private worship. I read once more the Old Testament prophecies and the New Testament story of the annunciation and Luke 2.

The new year brought more months of waiting for release. It also brought a roommate. In March permission was granted for Kathryn to join Ann Swift, the only other woman hostage. The two women had seen each other only once, at Christmastime, since the takeover in November. Armed with several versions of the Bible, they spent time reading and studying the Scriptures.

When Christmas rolled around again and found them still hostage, they planned together how to celebrate the festival. They used Christmas cards sent to them the year before to decorate their room. Kathryn folded paper to make a crèche. They fashioned an Advent wreath out of willow boughs. Each night they lit candles salvaged from earlier blackouts and had devotions together using hymns and scripture readings.

Surprisingly, the second Christmas as a hostage proved more difficult than the first. It seemed they were becoming more emotionally exhausted with each passing day. They were aware that the students would use the "Christmas festivities" for propaganda as they had the previous year and at Easter.

> Our worship services were important to us. We both missed our families but wanted very hard not to cry. I decided that we needed a good cry, so for the Christmas "sermon" I read a touching excerpt from *Bright Valley of Love.* This recounted an Advent/Christmas season in which a child comes to understand both the meaning of Christmas and the impending death of a playmate. We cried and laughed and cried. It got us over the hump.

Newscasts of the hostages were eagerly awaited by the millions of concerned Americans at home. That Christmas viewers sat spellbound as Kathryn sang the gentle lyrics:

> Be near me, Lord Jesus; I ask thee to stay
> Close by me forever, and love me, I pray.
> Bless all the dear children in thy tender care,
> And fit us for heaven, to live with thee there.

Commentators showed some confusion in identifying the song, but children and those who remembered the Christmases of their childhood knew it as the third stanza of "Away in a manger." Thinking of her nieces and nephews who might be terrified by what had happened to her, Kathryn chose that stanza of the familiar carol to assure them that she was all right. But beyond her own family the simple melody touched millions of others who were reminded once again of the Christ who came to bring peace to a confused and hostile world.

A few weeks later the 52 hostages were returned to the United States. They had spent 444 days in captivity. Throughout those days in Iran, Kathryn Koob offered a clear witness to her faith.

A long, long line of Christians has celebrated Christmas in hours of crisis. The festival still ministers the gracious gifts of God. In turn these persons have been a part of the legacy of courage and comfort, hope and help, strength and salvation with which God blesses his people. Their gifts were as varied as the precious gifts of the Wise Men. Their lives were a manifestation, an epiphany, of the grace of God at work. The shadows gathered them around the cross, and the Gift of the first Christmas was there.

Kathryn Koob

Christmas on Main Street

TEXT BY LEONARD FLACHMAN

ILLUSTRATIONS BY BOB ARTLEY

M ain Street took on a festive aura during the week before Christmas. Colored cellophane ropes draped the store windows. Small artificial wreaths, some with an electric candle in the center, hung from a few of the windows. Large red paper bells which had been folded away since last Christmas hung between the green ropes. Even the bank ventured a small pine tree on a table in the corner of the lobby.

Box of 36 9¢

On Main Street cutters, bobsleds, and autos were guided through the snow by those who had come to prepare for Christmas. The staccato sound of the automobile engines and the jingle of sleigh bells was highlighted by an occasional snort or whinny of a horse. The smell of wood smoke hung more heavily in the air.

The merchants put out the special Christmas merchandise that they had ordered weeks earlier. For this week the residents of the town and the surrounding farming communities would gather in the stores, exchanging Christmas

$2⁴⁹

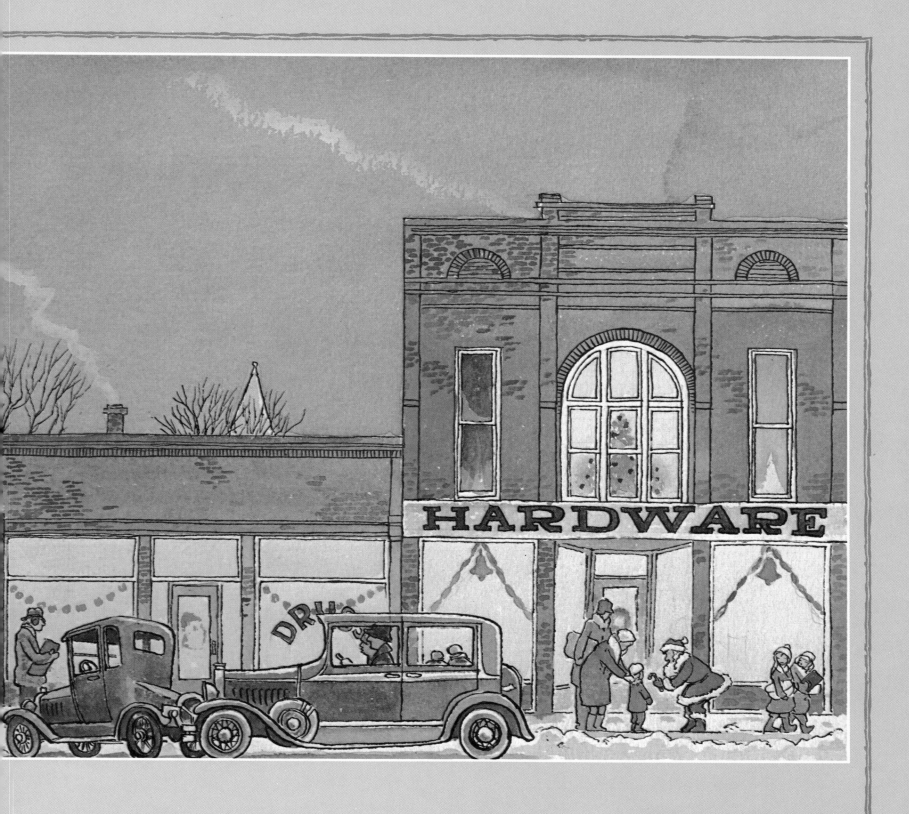

greetings. Their laughter and interest in purchasing a gift or two indicated that their visit to Main Street had a purpose other than their usual preoccupation with the necessities of life. All of Main Street took on the character of a Saturday night as the hustle and bustle increased during the week before Christmas.

Most of the local philosophers who sat around the wood stove in the grocery store, sharing idle thoughts and political de-

$1⁶⁹

bates, abdicated their stools. The discussions of comely womenfolk and the exaggerated hunting and fishing tales were postponed until after Christmas. Even the checker board sat empty in the corner near the stove. The families from the farms came to town to do some "trading." A few chickens with their legs tied together lay in the back of the bobsled. The cream can, not yet full, sat beside them.

$3⁷⁹

$1²⁵

FURNITURE and HOME APPLIANCES

Everyone in the family eyed the case of eggs covered with an old braided rug, but it was firmly established that the money from the eggs belonged to the farmer's wife.

The smell of the grocery store, suggesting cheese wedges, potatoes, and wheat flour became tinged with the aroma of

$1.29

39¢

spices and nuts, which were stocked for the convenience of the Christmas cooks. Through the sharp odor of cloves the children could quickly identify the smell of red and white striped peppermint candy canes.

In addition to the rock candy, horehound and peanut clusters were stocked for the festive season. Oranges in crates propped against the counter added bright color

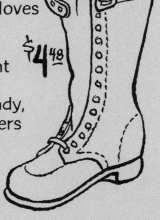

$4.48

to the usual array of coffee beans in bags beside the grinder, potatoes and onions in open cotton sacks, and summer sausages hanging from the ceiling over the counter. The usual items were in evidence in the hardware store. Rakes, shovels, pitchforks, and buggy whips hung along the walls. Popcorn poppers, pails, and other kitchen utensils hung from hooks in the ceiling. Not an inch of space was wasted. The green twisted crepe paper and red tissue bell in the window and the piles of tree top ornaments and electric Christmas tree lights seemed to be the only acknowledgment that Christmas was a week away.

Fancy hats replaced the front counter display of ribbon, colored braid, and buttons in the dry

$1⁶⁹

$2⁹⁸

$3⁴⁸

goods store. Piece goods by the bolt and fine gloves were featured in the "women's department." The "men's department" included celluloid collars, overalls, and red flannels. Mother, with a studied nonchalance, fingered a tie which she would later buy for father. And his face grew red as he picked up the bolts of bright calico. Both he and mother knew that he would come back later and buy the material which she had admired most.

Children, who were not permitted to accompany their parents into the stores, stood outside, their noses pressed against the

79¢ $1.19 $1.39

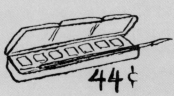

44¢

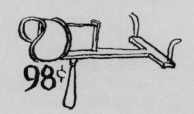

98¢

windows. They dreamed of all the exotic gifts they might receive this Christmas. Perhaps they would receive the wooden soldiers, the doll with the china head, or the tin horses in the window of the "5 & 10." Deep inside many of the children knew that after their parents had settled their accounts, there would be little cash money left. When Christmas came there would be candy and oranges for sure, and maybe, just maybe, their dreams would come true.

98¢

Each purchase was wrapped in brown paper pulled from a roller and torn against a sharp knife by the deft hand of the clerk. A seemingly endless supply of cord, from a cone-shaped ball under the ceiling, threaded its way into the hand of the clerk to tie and conceal the contents of the package.

By Christmas Eve all the bobsleds and autos were gone. The lights in the stores were turned off. The street was silent and dark. On Christmas Day a relaxed excitement was felt on Main Street as everyone gathered at the church. Not until next Christmas would Main Street take the character of Saturday night for a whole week.

To Louis at Christmas

ILIEN COFFEY

It's not just the sights of Christmas
That make it mean so much;
It's visits of friends and families and
The sounds and the smells and the touch.

The crinkly shell of a walnut
And the satiny smooth cashew—
They are nice to touch and nice to hear
As they snap when they crack in two.

The sound of the Christmas music
And the greetings we all repeat,
The sound of the crisp, cold snowflakes
As they crunch beneath your feet.

The smell of the turkey roasting,
The scent of a fresh-cut pine,
And the pictures you see with your fingertips
As you trace each new design.

The buttery taste of shortbread
And the warmth of the candle's glow;
The soft, round shape of a Mandarin orange
And the feel of a velvet bow.

It's not just the sights of Christmas
That makes it mean so much,
It's rejoicing again in the Savior's birth
And the sounds and the smells and the touch.

"To Louis at Christmas" was written by Ilien Coffey for her friend Louis, who is blind. Originally printed in Braille, the poem has been transcribed for sighted persons.

40

The Boxcar Pilgrim

PAT CORRICK HINTON

The long hallway of the nursing home was bright with holly and big red bows. It raised our spirits from the rainy chill outside, so characteristic of Christmastime in Oregon. My two young children and I walked quickly to Room 108, hoping to spread some cheer to this first lonely resident on our list.

I knocked, leaned in, and called, "Mr. Brown? Are you there?"

A tall, thin man with gray hair and very red cheeks rose from the edge of the bed and hobbled over to us.

"Yes'm. Brown's m' name, but I'd rather you call me Bill. I may be a bum, but I'm still a gentleman." With that he gave a little bow and then squeezed rather than shook each of our hands very firmly and invited us to come over to his cubicle.

Sitting down he abruptly put one foot up on the bed and said, "Looky here, kiddies. I've got somethin' to show ya." He yanked off a sock so we could see an enormous foot with a purplish space where three toes used to be.

David and all his 10 years gasped right out loud, and Annie hid her face in my coat. We felt repulsed and curi-ous at the same time and moved forward for a little better look. Bill seemed to enjoy our reactions because he went right on: "See how my foot is healing? Got it jammed in a railroad hitch last month," he said rather proudly. "Good thing it was my feet and not my hands."

"Oh-uh, you travel by railroad, Bill?" I asked with a quiver in my voice.

"You bet I'm a traveler, ma'am." He chuckled. "Yep. That's it. A professional traveler, on my way to the Prom-ised Land, only it don't cost me nothin'. When I get hungry I make and sell one of these." Bill took something from the top of his nightstand. It was a figure of a dog, a retriever. It was carved out of wood, and it was beautiful.

"Bill," I said in amazement, "you *made* this?"

"Sure did. You might say that's how I make my livin'— travelin' around the country and selling my pets here. You can see why it's a good thing I lost some toes instead of my fingers. Hobblin' is better than not eatin'."

David had a million questions: "Do you really travel all the time?" "Where do you go?" "Where do you sleep?"

41

"Who buys your carvings?" and especially, "How'd you get your foot caught so bad?"

Bill chuckled again and drew Annie and David to each side of him. He motioned me to sit on the chair. "Well, now, that's a lot of questions to be answerin'. Is it the big cities you want to know about or the wide open spaces?" And off he went, taking us with him on his boxcar travels, filling our imaginations with vivid pictures. The more Bill talked the more excited and red in the face he became. His sharp features lit up as he gestured with his hands to describe how *huge* the buildings were in New York or Chicago and how *wide* the oceans and Great Lakes were. He tapped with his fingers to show the monotonous sound of the clicking boxcars on the tracks. We could easily imagine him whittling away on a block of wood as the train whipped across the country.

Finally, as he began to wind down, he said, "I'd be out there still if I hadn't been so careless and fallen between those two boxcars and gotten my old foot stuck. Sure did hurt. They were so tight in that hitch I couldn't budge 'em a bit. Just had to hang there until somebody came along and got me loose. Even heard the bones crack! Then, o' course when they got me in the hospital they figured them toes weren't no good anymore so they chopped 'em off."

I cringed at the thought of this, but Bill said, "Oh, no mind, ma'am. I couldn'ta used 'em anyhow. Kinda strange without 'em, but I'm gettin' used to it. See? He inched off the bed and limped a few steps to show us how well he could walk.

Annie and David plied him with questions until I said we really had to leave. Bill begged us to visit him again, promising more adventure stories. We promised to return.

We spent the next few days baking cookies in the shapes of trees, wreaths, stars, and candy canes. Bill popped up in our conversation continually. As the children became more adept at turning out nearly-perfect shapes, I would hear: "Look, Mom. This one's for Bill." Or, "Hey, Mom, won't Bill just love this star?" As we packed the last cookie that could possibly fit in a decorative tin for Bill, David said, "I hope he doesn't eat all these right away. He might need some when he takes another big trip. Boy, I hope I can explore the whole world someday just like Bill does." And David's thoughts, I'm sure, rambled off with Bill in a boxcar.

Annie taped a red bow on the top of the cookie tin and begged, "Please, Mom, do we have to wait till Christmas to take these cookies to Bill? Can't we take them over right now?" David joined in the begging and I couldn't think of a reason not to go that afternoon. When we arrived we were shocked by his news. His recovery was complete, and he would be leaving the nursing home the day after New Years to visit his brother back east in Pennsylvania.

"It's time I saw a little country again. I get kinda itchy if I'm in one place too long. Anyways, I haven't seen my brother for a long, long time."

I gripped David's shoulder. I had a feeling that he was secretly wishing Bill could come and stay with us so we could listen to his stories forever. I had a lump in my throat as I said, "Bill, we're happy you're recovering so well, but that's a long distance from here to Pennsylvania. Do you have everything you need? Do you have a warm coat? You'll be going through the cold Midwest." Being originally from Minnesota, I knew just how cold it could get.

Bill shifted from one foot to the other admitting finally, "Well, ma'am. Guess I could use a coat of some kind. You're right. It gets cold out that way and the one I been wearin' isn't much of a coat anymore."

On the way home David said, "Mom, I'll just bet Bill needs more than a coat. Can't we get him some other clothes too?"

"Yes, yes," shouted Annie, jumping up and down on the seat. "Let's get him some shirts and pants and sweaters and socks and gloves and. . . ."

"Whoa, just a minute, kids," I said. "We have to remember Bill travels pretty light so let's try to get him the things he might need most."

As Christmas drew nearer, all of us, including my husband who hadn't yet met Bill, were caught up in the excitement of helping him prepare for his new adventure. Jim found a hat, and some friends donated two almost new shirts. In the middle of this search David made a decision. "All this stuff we're giving Bill is *used*. Can I give him something brand new for a Christmas present?"

"That's a nice idea, David," I said. "What do you have in mind?"

"I can make him a belt from that kit with the leather loops."

"And *I'll* make him a bee-oootiful card," said Annie.

And so began a lovely accumulation of nice things for our friend Bill. But the coat was a problem. We inquired and looked everywhere with no luck. Heavy coats simply weren't needed in Oregon winters.

Finally, on Christmas Eve, around 4:00, we were wrapping Bill's gifts to take over the next day.

"I just hate to tell Bill we couldn't find a coat for him," I said.

"Well, let's tell him we're still looking," said my husband. "Somebody must have one packed away somewhere. Wait a minute! I think I just might know . . . ." And suddenly he was gone out to the garage and was moving boxes and bikes, making a great racket.

Many minutes later he came puffing into the kitchen, flushed and grinning. "I had one packed away somewhere and forgot I had it. Guess we've been out in the moderate West too long!"

The children oh-ed and ah-ed over the coat, but I said, "Jim, this is a beautiful coat and almost new."

"Yes, it is. I have two, and if we ever get back to the Midwest, I'll still have one to wear," he declared.

What a Christmas Eve we had! Preparing to share our goods with our gentle new friend who owned so little, then making a huge Christmas card with the words from Luke: "If you have two coats, give one to the poor." Inside we printed: "Merry, merry Christmas, Dad. We're proud of you." And we were so proud of him. He not only shared his coat. He gave away the best one!

We each had a gift to bring Bill on Christmas Day. As we gathered with giggles and "Merry Christmas" in the doorway of his room, his face lit up with an enormous smile. He limped toward us, arms outstretched. "Well, and Merry Christmas to you all. Am I glad to see you folks. And you must be the mister," Bill said as he squeezed my husband's one free hand. "Come in, come in so's I can have a better look at ya. My, my, what *is* all this?" said Bill as we handed him our gifts. Jim stood behind me still holding the coat camouflaged under a plastic cleaners bag. Carefully Bill set the boxes on the bed.

"Open mine first, Bill," said Annie excitedly, holding it almost in his face. "Do you want me to help you? I made the card myself!"

Bill sat there chuckling as Annie ripped the paper from the carefully wrapped shirts. "Well, now, don't that beat all, honey. Those are real shirts! And who might this be on your card here, that good lookin' feller ridin' the boxcar?"

"It's *you*, Bill, it's you!" Annie giggled.

"Oh, and look at this swell hat. My, my, this is grand. Now what you got here, sonny? Well, well. Real nice work," Bill said as he examined and tried on the belt. "You like to work with your hands too, eh, sonny? I can tell it's handmade. Real nice work." As he stood up the belt sagged a little.

David started to say something, but Annie burst in, "And he made it all by himself, Bill. Just for you!"

David grinned and said, "Now here's the big one, Bill. Here's your really *big* present!" Jim held the hanger while both children scrambled to lift the plastic covering. Bill's eyes grew wide as he took in the black and gray and white tweed coat with a big red bow in the lapel. "Merry Christmas, Bill!" we said again.

Bill was suddenly speechless, perhaps for the first time in his life. His eyes filled and he shook his head, saying over and over, "Oh, my goodness. Well, and thank you, ma'am, and thank you, sir. Oh, and thank you, kiddies.

I just never had such a beautiful coat in my whole entire life. Oh, I do thank you. My, my . . . . " He touched the coat gently with his long fingers.

Our eyes filled too. Annie was the only one who could say what we were thinking. She said simply, "I like you, Bill. Can we always be your friends?"

Bill touched her cheek and said, "Oh, you betcha, honey. I bet you're just about the best friends I got."

On New Year's Day we visited Bill for the last time. Each of us felt we were losing a friend, but Bill was so excited we didn't dare seem gloomy.

I said, "We'd like to know how you're getting along, Bill, so here's our name and address. Won't you drop us a line every so often?"

Bill said he would and tucked the small piece of paper into his wallet. He squeezed our hands tightly and touched Annie's cheek again. As he came to David he reached into his shirt pocket and took out the carved retriever we'd seen the first day we met him. "This is for all of you, but I want *you* to be in charge of it. Maybe it'll give you a little thought of me while I'm travelin' around." He paused and winked at David. "Be a good boy, sonny. Until we meet again."

We continued to visit the nursing home after Bill left, but it was never quite the same. And then time changed everything.

Nine months later my husband transferred back to Minnesota. We were all busy getting acquainted and re-acquainted with relatives and friends when an air mail letter arrived, forwarded from our Oregon home. The return address was a funeral home in Kankakee, Illinois. It read: "On September 10, 1972, Mr. William R. Brown passed away while traveling through Kankakee. If you can be of any help in the location of information and/or relatives, please call or write us. We are requesting this of you because in Mr. Brown's billfold he had a piece of paper with your name and address, with the words, 'These are my only friends.'"

Rest in peace, Bill. Until we meet again.

Christmas Butterfly

SUSAN R. IDE

Christmas is a butterfly unfolding
From winter's chrysalis. Out of the black
And white December harshness flash colors,
Soft fragilities of wings. Icy streets
Shine red and green and gold. Scarlet and pink
Poinsettias glow by hearths. Angels abound.
Christmas is a butterfly unfolding
From the cold human heart. Out of the bleak

Preoccupation with our private woes
And wants, out of the tedium of routines,
There springs the wish to give and to forgive.
Love once again believes and hopes all things.
That Christmas comes each year is proof enough:
Miracles of birth and rebirth still occur.

Royal Sages

Polish, tr. Felician Sisters

Polish, arr. Carolyn Jennings

1. Roy ~ al sa ~ ges from a ~ far, pray whith ~ er leads your
1. Mędr ~ cy świa ~ ta, mo ~ nar ~ cho ~ wie, gdzie spiesz ~ nie dą ~
2. Roy ~ al sa ~ ges, cru ~ el fu ~ ry is the child pur ~

quest ~ ing? Seek ye here the new ~ ly born in yon ~ der man ~ ger
ży ~ cie? Po ~ wiedz ~ cież nam, trzej Kró ~ lo ~ wie, chce ~ cie wi ~ dzieć
su ~ ing, Bad the news and sad the tid ~ ings: Her ~ od's wick ~ ed

rest ~ ing? Poor and low ~ ly lies the In ~ fant,
Dzie ~ cię? O ~ no w żło ~ bie, nie ma tro ~ nu,
plans bring. But the Wise Men ev ~ er fear ~ less,

throne nor scep ~ ter claim ~ ing. Yet to all his
ni ber ~ ła nie dzierż ~ y, A pro ~ ro ~ ctwo
bear ~ ing gifts from far . . Has ~ ten to the

sav ~ ing death in proph ~ e ~ cy pro ~ claim ~ ing.
Je ~ go zgo ~ nu już się w świe ~ cie sze ~ rzy.
hum ~ ble sta ~ ble, guid ~ ed by the bright star.

Infant Holy, Infant Lowly

Polish, tr. Edith M.G. Reed,
Zofia Kowalska McGinn

Polish, arr. Richard W. Hillert

*In - fant ho - ly, in - fant low - ly, For his bed a cat - tle stall;
1. Wżło - bie le - ży! ktòż po - bie - ży Ko - lę - do - wać ma - łe - mu
1. In a man-ger sleeps the In - fant, Has-ten all to find him there.

Ox - en low-ing, lit-tle know-ing Christ the child is Lord of all.
Je - zu - so - wi Chry-stu - so - wi Dziś do nas ze-sła - ne - mu?
Lit - tle Je - sus, to us heav'n sent, Bless-ings with us all to share.

Swift-ly wing-ing, an-gels sing-ing, Bells are ring-ing, tid-ings bring-ing:
Pa - stu - szko - wie przy - by - waj - cie, Je - mu wdzię-cznie przy-gry-waj - cie,
Hur - ry, shep - herds, kneel be - fore him, Like the an - gels praise, a - dore him;

Christ the child is Lord of all! Christ the child is Lord of all!
Ja - ko Pa - nu na-sze - mu, Ja - ko Pa - nu na-sze - mu.
Wor - ship him as Lord and King. Wor - ship him as Lord and King.

46

* Although not a direct translation of the Polish text, this stanza is often sung with this charming Polish tune.

Quickly on to Bethlehem

Polish, tr. Cecily Kowalewska Helgesen

Polish, arr. Sam Batt Owens

1. Quick-ly on to Beth-le-hem the shep-herds came, Play-ing gai-ly
1. Przy-bie-że-li do Be-tle-jem pas-te-rze, Gra-jąc skocz-nie
2. Giv-ing their re-spects in all hu-mil-i-ty Shep-herds came to

on their lutes to bless his name. Glo-ry to God in heav-en, Glo-ry to
Dzie-cią-tecz-ku na li-rze. Chwa-ła na wy-so-koś-ci, Chwa-ła na
wor-ship him on bend-ed knee. Glo-ry to God in heav-en, Glo-ry to

God in heav-en And on earth, peace to men.
wy-so-koś-ci, A po-kój na zie-mi.
God in heav-en And on earth, peace to men.

In Bethlehem

Polish, tr. Cecily Kowalewska Helgesen

Polish, arr. Charles W. Ore

1. In Beth-le-hem,.. in Beth-le-hem,.. Tid-ings ring tri-
1. Dzi-siaj w Be-tle-jem, dzi-siaj w Be-tle-jem, We-so-ła no-
2. Sweet vir-gin Mar-y, Sweet vir-gin Mar-y O'er her wee babe

um-phant! Sweet vir-gin Mar-y sweet vir-gin Mar-y
wi-na! Że Pan-na czys-ta, że Pan-na czys-ta
bend-ing, And kind-ly Jo-seph, and kind-ly Jo-seph

Bore the ho-ly In-fant. Born is our Sav-ior, born our Re-deem-er,
po-ro-dzi-ła Sy-na. Chrys-tus się ro-dzi, Nas os-wo-bo-dzi,
Gent-ly them at-tend-ing. Born is our Sav-ior, born our Re-deem-er,

An-gels are play-ing, Kings trib-ute pay-ing, Shep-herds all are sing-ing,
A-nie-li gra-ją, Kró-le wi-ta-ją, Pas-te-rze śpie-wa-ją,
An-gels are play-ing, Kings trib-ute pay-ing, Shep-herds all are sing-ing,

Sheep and ox-en kneel-ing, Lo! what won-der! Each pro-claim-ing.
Byd-lę-ta klę-ka-ją, Cu-da, cu-da! O-gła-sza-ją.
Sheep and ox-en kneel-ing, Lo! what won-der! Each pro-claim-ing.

Lullaby, Sweet Jesus

Polish, tr. Evelyn Nahurski

Polish, arr. Robert Wetzler

1. Lul - la - by, sweet Je - sus, pearl ver - y
1. Lu - laj - że, Je - zu - niu, mo - ja pe -
2. Close now your wee eye - lids, blink - ing with

pre - cious. Lul - la - by, sweet Je - sus,
ret - ko, Lu - laj - że, Je - zu - niu,
soft tears; Still your wee lips trem - bling,

sleep now, your cries hush. Lul - la - by,
me pie - ści - deł - ko, Lu - laj - że,
for slum - ber time nears. Lul - la - by,

sweet Je - sus, lul - la - by, ba - by,
Je - zu - niu, lu - laj - że, lu - laj,
sweet Je - sus, lul - la - by, ba - by,

In - fant be - lov - ed, your moth - er will lull thee.
A Ty Go Ma - tu - chno w pła - czu u - tu - laj.
In - fant be - lov - ed, your moth - er will lull thee.

Manhattan Christmas

ROBERT E. A. LEE

You can't be in the heart of New York City in December without feeling Christmas. You see it in the theatrical lighting, you hear it in the contrapuntal cacaphony of carols against the clamor of commerce, you smell it in the alien aroma of pine and fir, and you can even taste it in the delicacies dispersed from the collective cultures of the world.

Manhattan is a curious setting for a Christmas festival. It seems as if the values of the human race are all jammed together on these sometimes mean streets along with the cosmopolitan contradictions that resettled tribes and transient visitors imported once upon a time.

New York is a secular, congested, dirty city. But it's much more than that. It's also the cultural and commercial center of the universe. It is said that almost anything you need or want in the world is available somewhere in New York City, if only you have the time and talent to find it. Certainly it is one of the most exciting cities on the planet—especially at Christmas!

A December visitor flying into La-Guardia airport may, if lucky, look down on a clear night to see the Empire State Building pushing its Christmas message up to and sometimes through the clouds. The venerable skyscraper (over a half-century old) is seasonally aglow with green and white lights, accented by twinking, tip-top red ones as if to simulate a giant Christmas tree. Nearby in the same urban forest of stone tapers, the Metropolitan Life tower has its illuminated clock wreathed in red and its peak outlined in Christmas-tree green.

A visitor by train may emerge from the tracks below Penn Station to the sounds of Christmas as commuters linger in the waiting room to sing along with the electric organ accompaniments played fortissimo by a

Photo: Empire State Building.

ruddy faced, red-headed Long Island Railroad engineer, known best by his obvious nickname, "Red." Up the escalator and outside, a Salvation Army uniformed brass quartet plays on the consciences of passers-by for alms.

If you had only a few minutes to experience Christmastime in Manhattan, you would probably do what countless tourists do—hurry to Rockefeller Center to capture there the visual memory of the legendary Christmas tree that graces the plaza. It's quite a sight as millions have discovered by the television coverage of its lighting ceremony. A 65-foot Norwegian spruce laden with thousands of multi-colored lights, it stands sentry beneath the tower of the RCA building and watches over the holiday skaters on the plaza ice rink below.

To share the view, to see the lucky few gliding on the white glaze, you need to push through the throng of onlookers leaning over the railing. There's always an audience of down-jacketed children hand-held by patronizing parents. You walk behind them, perhaps marching a bit to the music of one of the many visiting high school bands, and edge your way up through the Channel Gardens to Fifth Avenue. On the way you pass the wire-sculptured clusters of trumpeting angels and sunbursts, festively lighted. With camera in hand you seek the best vantage point for the mandatory picture. Once there, you focus on a picture-postcard sight: the mighty tree standing at the far end of an alley of fantasy. For many, Christmas in Manhattan would not be Christmas without the symbolism of that tree.

Every town has its Christmas trees and decorations and those in Manhattan may not surpass any elsewhere. But in the midst of the concrete canyons of this Babylon on the Hudson, the festooned evergreens seem to stand more starkly as a statement of hope to congregated humanity.

At City Hall, downtown at Broadway and Park Place, there's an official tree, a 55-foot fir. It's one of over three dozen donated to the city by the International Paper Company. A chorus of school children sings at the lighting ceremony at dusk on an early December day. As always in New York, when school children sing

Christmas songs they also include the several that commemorate the Jewish festival of Hanukkah.

Because New York has more Jews than even Israel, there is some attempt made to give Hanukkah "equal time" with Christmas. Merchants promote gift giving for both occasions and their greetings to customers play it safe with the neutral slogan, "Happy Holidays." Jews themselves recognize the Judas Maccabeus memorial event of 165 B.C. only as a minor festival. Christian neighbors of New York's large Jewish population seem more and more to understand the need for respecting the Hanukkah symbolism of the menorah as culturally and religiously complementary to their Christmas festival.

There are unusual trees at two of Manhattan's major museums. An Origami holiday tree is traditional at the Museum of Natural History on Central Park West. Three thousand hand-folded paper ornaments, in the Japanese style, decorate a 25-foot Scotch pine. On the other (Fifth Avenue) side of the park, a 20-foot spruce has been decorated at the Metropolitan Museum of Art. Baroque angels and cherubs cover the tree. At its base are dozens of crèche figures about a foot tall. Most of them are from Naples and date from the mid-18th century. Their pliable bodies, woven from twine and wire, allow them to be positioned in tableaux. The heads and limbs of the figures are of finely carved wood. Elegant costumes, many with jewels, were made for the crèche figures by Italian noblewomen of the period.

For all of its adult sophistication, Christmas in Manhattan really deserves to be seen through the eyes of children. This is one time of the year when you may be especially rewarded by taking a child in each hand (grandchildren are excellent for this purpose) to explore the sights until you or they are exhausted.

An ideal time is a Sunday between 10:00 A.M. and 3:00 P.M., and the ideal place is Fifth Avenue between 34th Street and 57th Street. The Fifth Avenue Holiday Festival has become a tradition. The thoroughfare is closed to traffic and its use as a pedestrian mall provides its own festive charm.

Photos: Rockefeller Center.

Photos: Washington Place, horse-drawn carriage in Central Park, Washington Square, street vendor selling hot pretzels and roasted chestnuts, shoppers resting on the steps of St. Patrick's Cathedral.

Amusement stations have been provided at intervals along the avenue. Walking uptown from the Empire State Building at 34th Street, you will first discover a Skatemobile where the children can flex their legs on a mini-rink. Continuing your walk northbound to 41st Street, you can smile at the sculptured lions guarding the New York Public Library. Today they have Christmas wreaths around their necks. A little farther on at 44th Street, the children will be entranced by the little show at the Marionettemobile.

Street musicians abound in Manhattan at Christmastime. They range from the ubiquitous Salvation Army brass ensembles (with a kettle but not a drum) to a flute, bassoon, and clarinet trio to an electric guitarist to a steel band. Their songs run the gamut from "Winter Wonderland" to familiar carols to Vivaldi and Bach. With luck you might arrive at Rockefeller Plaza in time to hear the rare sound of a band of 500 tubas!

As you approach St. Patrick's Cathedral a choir may be singing on the steps. Go inside to rest and share the sense of awe that interior gives. Along the side aisles you will see hundreds of red votive lights. By the baptismal font a manger has been set up with statues representing the original Bethlehem cast. Poinsettia plants are everywhere.

Outside, it's time to head downtown again with the children. They must see the special windows in department stores. On the way you meet multiple copies of Santa Claus, each with his bell calling for contributions on behalf of the Volunteers of America Christmas dinner project. A blind beggar with a guide dog has his own fund raising project; he wears a sign that says, "God Bless the Cheerful Giver."

Panhandlers, including the pathetic bag ladies with their scavenged possessions in shopping bags, emerge on the streets in even greater numbers right before Christmas. They compete with the peddlers for pedestrian dollars. You can buy costume jewelry, gloves, caps, and assorted other Christmas stocking trinkets.

It's hard to resist the hawkers of hot pretzels—a street staple in Manhattan—or a bag of hand-warming hot chestnuts roasted over charcoal.

Whether the motivation is commercial, cultural, or Christian, everyone on the sidewalks of New York tries to get into the act at Christmas. Even the official airline of the Soviet Union has a decorated tree in the window of its Aeroflot offices on Fifth Avenue at 45th Street.

Lord and Taylor's windows at 39th Street are extraordinary by any standards. You'll need to go around the block and join a queue of other curious young and old and wait maybe 10 minutes for your passage inside the roped-off section under the awnings. Your reward will be a series of animated tableaux depicting Christmas celebrations in various centuries in New York going back to the days of Peter Stuyvesant. Each is like an elegant miniature movie set with lifelike dolls moving smoothly like automatons through Manhattan's history as Christmas was observed way back when. One year the theme will be show business including famous theatrical and operatic productions of the past; in another year the motif may be transportation or dinner parties. Adults probably appreciate these windows more than children.

At Altman's store at 34th Street, however, the window messages are more nearly calculated to win the hearts of the very young. Always there is a story, usually with animated animals, and each window displays a separate episode that connects with the others whether the onlookers move along from left to right or from right to left. A recorded voice provides a narrative. Children will linger to laugh and point at something funny they've discovered while adults will foolishly try to take flash pictures through the highly reflective glass.

If you were shopping for free visual delights, the Fifth Avenue Festival was only a beginning. Over on Park Avenue you will find the modernistic glass building, Lever House. In its corner street-level showroom a fully operative carousel has been placed and on it fancily dressed manikins ride endlessly in circles.

A view up Park Avenue at the center boulevard's parade of white-lighted Christmas trees is impressive, especially at twilight. Last spring

this same floral mile was abloom with Easter lilies; they will return again next spring.

Far uptown near the tip of Manhattan Island at Fort Tryon Park, the Cloisters contain a remarkable horticultural and art display. The Romanesque chapel is a place you can rest and meditate while listening to early Yuletide music and looking at the greenery adorning the ancient altar canopy. Mixed with the musty aroma of the imported stonework and masonry is the scent of the swags of pine and cedar and the garlands of herbs and spicy fruits. In nearby chambers you can admire 15th century Florentine terra-cotta figures from the famed workshop of Antonio Rossellino.

At the other downtown tip of the island your mind and perspective will leap centuries as you contemplate the present and future symbolism of the twin towers of the World Trade Center. At night, weather permitting, virtually all of Christmas-lit Manhattan is spread out before you as you look northward from the 110th floor observation deck. Turning eastward, your view includes planes landing at La-Guardia with Christmas-bound passengers, the twin bridges of Whitestone and Throgs Neck with their distant lights outlining Christmas-tree-like patterns, and then Queens and Brooklyn with their bridges and airports. A kinetic web of traffic moves in a chain of headlights through parkways and streets to millions of homes. Some residential areas glow with colored lights.

Not all of the Christmas wonder of the World Trade Center is at the top. On the ground floor of Tower One you may find a charming toy railroad display that is called the "Gingerbread Express," while the lobby of Tower Two may provide a puppet show for children at scheduled hours during the day.

Puppets and dolls and toys of all kinds add a playful touch to Christmas for children whether purchased, wished for, or only on display. The New York Historical Society has a permanent exhibition of playthings, dolls, miniature furniture and tableware, cast-iron and tin vehicles. A Queen Anne-type doll from Germany dates back to the late 18th century.

Today's toys, however, are likely to be animated and automated, many

of them battery operated. The battery division of the Union Carbide Corporation (Park Avenue at 48th Street) has a display on its mezzanine floor that is sure to excite young children. Lights blink and flash, miniature machines move with a magical meter, cars and trucks and jeeps and space buggies careen crazily around the room with electric abandon.

Perhaps the ultimate toyland is the F.A.O. Schwartz store on upper Fifth Avenue. Kids can fantasize over doll houses and stuffed toys, and many may covet one of the motorized mini-Mercedes sports cars. More modest toy towns can be found near Herald Square at Macy's and Gimbels. Here and at almost every other large department store you'll find a queue leading to Santa's lap.

Another almost mandatory queue for families in Manhattan at Christmastime is the line-up outside the Radio City Music Hall. Called "The Magnificent Christmas Spectacular," it lives up to its description. Over 100 performers sing and dance and theatrically cavort on the huge stage. For many years the show stopper was the parade of camels and other live animals on the way to the Bethlehem manger. Now there is a multimedia version of "The 12 Days of Christmas" and a delightful staging of "A Visit from St. Nicholas." The high-kicking Rockettes are a perennial favorite. The Corps de Ballet offers a scaled down adaptation of *The Nutcracker Suite* and, after the lush prelude from the grand theater organ, the symphony orchestra rises dramatically from the pit. The centerpiece remains a nativity pageant bathed in blue light. A menorah, however, is lighted also so that the show can at least give a token salute to Hanukkah.

Manhattan has a magnetism for lovers of theater. All through December and into January, seasonal entertainment seekers are drawn to the city. They come from the other boroughs, from Long Island, from Westchester County and New Jersey to join tourists and holiday-liberated students and school children at concerts, operas, ballets, plays, and special programs. Most events are "off Broadway." Many are hosted by churches. Offerings in recent years have included the following.

Photos: crowds enjoying the store windows.

• *The Nutcracker Suite* by the New York City Ballet is a tradition, a popular annual Christmastime ritual for children. The dreamy charm of its dancers and the lilting melodies of Tchaikovsky's enchanting score have made it a favorite.

• *Hansel and Gretel* is a perennial children's event at the Metropolitan Opera on Christmas Eve and Christmas night. The staging for this 1893 work by Engelbert Humperdinck includes an incomparably tantalizing gingerbread house.

• *Babes in Toyland* by Victor Herbert, presented by the Light Opera of Manhattan, is a melodic morality play about a toymaker and his helpers. While other of the composer's operettas have lost popular appeal, this one lives on through the strength of its seasonal revivals.

• *Amahl and the Night Visitors* by Gian Carlo Menotti is always presented somewhere in Manhattan each Christmas. A recent season found it in at least three locations the same weekend.

• *A Christmas Carol* by Dickens survives annually in several Manhattan versions. Trinity Lutheran Church on the upper West Side at 100th Street has fashioned a musical version entitled "Mr. Scrooge," with the pastor's daughter cast as Tiny Tim. Other adaptions include the Ridiculous Theatrical Company's performance of Charles Ludlam's script at Sheridan Square and Shelter West's performance of Shaun Sutton's script at the Nameless Theater on 22nd Street West.

• *Christmas Rappings*, the Nativity story in modern dress, is one of the most recent productions created by Al Carmines and staged by him at the church on Washington Square where he is one of the ministers. Carmine's earlier revue, "The Last Christmas Elf," has entertained customers at the Manhattan Savings Bank at Madison Avenue and 47th Street.

Free concerts at other commercial establishments, especially at noontime, can be found almost daily in the heart of the city. The well-blended voices of a mixed sextet echo through the lobby of the Pan Am Building, catching pedestrians and commuters on their way to or from the escalators leading to Grand Central Station. The singers avoid the more familiar Christmas carols and instead offer baroque songs from the 17th and 18th centuries.

In the modernistic atrium of the Citicorp Center at Lexington and 54th Street, you could hear "The Jazz Nativity," carols sung in the jazz idiom with 10 singers and actors. This is an extension of the jazz ministry of St. Peter's Lutheran Church that is built into the northwest corner of the center. The program is presented also in the sanctuary of the church and includes a Christmas carol version of Duke Ellington's composition, "Come Sunday."

Another equally different production of the Christmas story is Langston Hughes' "Black Nativity." You may find it at the Richard Allen Center for Culture and Art on West 62nd Street near Lincoln Center where it was revived several years ago. The well-known black author and poet, who died in 1967, first introduced it on Broadway over 20 years ago as a production involving mime, gospel, spirituals, dance, and dialog. "Black Nativity" traveled widely over Western Europe and across the United States and met enthusiastic acclaim. Now it may join other seasonal classics in becoming a New York tradition.

No city's Christmas is complete without a performance of George Friedrich Handel's oratorio, the *Messiah*. In Manhattan you'll have your choice of many presentations to listen to and even one or two where the audience comes to sing. For example, at Avery Fisher Hall there is an annual *Messiah* sing-in. Please bring your own score if you have one (they are for sale in the lobby) and join the other 3000 voices. Imagine the volume of the Hallelujah Chorus or the final amen! The National Choral Council has arranged to have 21 conductors deployed throughout the auditorium, each responsible for a section. They take their beat from the head maestro on center stage, where he is surrounded by the professional soloists and the organist.

In addition to *Messiah* performances in churches, you'll find annual concerts by the Masterwork Chorus and Orchestra, directed by David Randolph (who also has a sing-along event), and by the Oratorio Society of New York, which first presented the Handel work in 1873.

You'll also have a choice of several presentations in Manhattan of *The Christmas Oratorio* by Johann Sebastian Bach. In some concert halls an evening will be devoted to the entire work consisting of six cantatas. Most churches where it is sung select Part I for Christmas Eve, as Bach intended, or Part II for Christmas Day.

A glance at the ambitious musical calendar for Christmas week in New York will tell you that other popular offerings are Benjamin Britten's *A Ceremony of Carols,* Bach's *Magnificat,* Sant-Saên's *Christmas Oratorio,* Vaughan Williams's *The First Nowell,* and Vivaldi's *Gloria.*

The renaissance of early music that is sweeping the world is particularly apparent in the concert listings and church notices in New York City. The Waverly Consort, reviving an ancient setting of the Christmas story with narrator, costumed singers, and musicians playing antique instruments, finds its concerts at the Metropolitan Museum of Art often sold out. Similarly, the Ensemble for Early Music, performing 13th to 17th century English and Scottish seasonal music, will fill Alice Tully Hall at Lincoln Center. There is a quality of sound to the lute, vielle, sackbut, shawm, and cornetto that evokes a mysterious linkage between our Christmas today and observances of centuries past. These strange, somewhat strident, and often eerie harmonics find sympathetic acoustics in vaulted churches; in various New York congregations the disciples of early music will find Advent and Christmas offerings especially rewarding.

An even more complete early music experience is offered by St. George's Chapel on East 16th Street. By attending their Renaissance Christmas, you can not only enjoy music performed by costumed musicians and watch clowns, jugglers, and dancers but also feast on a festive meal of roast suckling pig. If you've never before been close to a wassail bowl, here's your chance to taste its spicy nectar.

Yuletide music is not heard only inside churches, museums, and concert halls. The famous bells of the Riverside Church peal familiar carols from its tower high above the

Hudson River on Morningside Heights. The carillonneur, James R. Lawson, performs daily at noon and also invites others from among the relatively few carillon players of the world to come to Riverside during the Christmas season to give guest concerts.

How would you like to troupe through the streets of Greenwich Village singing carols? You can, as a part of the annual caroling walk organized by the West Village Chorale. On one of the nights before Christmas anyone interested can gather at the Church of St. Luke in the Fields at 7:30, choose one of two prescribed routes through the Village and, after the walk, return to the church for refreshments.

For 46 years one of the most exciting and different seasonal experiences has been the "Star of Wonder" presentation at the Hayden Planetarium at the American Museum of Natural History on Central Park West at 79th Street. On the domed ceiling the planetarium has recreated the look of the sky in Bethlehem at the time of the birth of Jesus. There are two performances each afternoon.

Your Christmas in New York City will climax on Christmas Eve. Don't plan on snow. Only every four or five years is the Big Apple (NYC's nickname) treated to a white Christmas. But it may be cold and damp and windy.

Because it gets dark early, many church services begin at 4:30 or 5:00. That schedule is preferred by many who want to spend the balance of the evening with families. The elderly often want to avoid being on the streets late at night.

The late hour, however—10:30 or 11:00 or even midnight—has a certain dramatic appeal for the worshiper who associates Christmas Eve with the exhilaration of the angel choir's "Gloria" that first Christmas night.

Come along to a Christmas Eve worship experience in Manhattan! Almost every Christian church is open for business. Come early if you want a seat.

One possibility among many is to attend the service at the Evangelical Lutheran Church of the Holy Trinity

Photos: Citicorp Center, tuba choir at Rockefeller Center, Pan Am Building.

on Central Park West at 65th Street. This is the famous Bach church in New York where the cantatas of Johann Sebastian Bach are offered by the church's Bach choir and orchestra at Sunday afternoon Vespers from November through April except during Advent and Lent. You discover that the Holy Trinity musicians are offering Bach's *The Christmas Oratorio* (Part I) as a half-hour prelude to the Holy Communion service that begins at 11:00 on Christmas Eve.

You arrive shortly before 10:00 to be sure you'll get a seat and in order not to miss the oratorio. But the doors are locked. You wait in the cold. Others come and huddle outside on the steps with you. Soon there is a small congregation of Christmas pilgrims sharing both their impatience and their heightened sense of expectancy. Waiting there gives you time to notice across the street in Central Park that the barren, leafless branches of the trees nearest the street and adjacent to Tavern on the Green are festooned with thousands of tiny white lights.

Suddenly an usher opens the huge front doors of the church. As if acting out the symbolic drama of Advent— waiting, watching, anticipating—the faithful enter the prepared holy space to seek and to find Christmas.

The church is dimly lit. You choose a pew toward the front so that the music from the rear balcony can reach you with full effect. As you wait in whispered silence your eyes are drawn to the mosaic panels behind the ornate white altar.

Then Bach. The oratorio music sets the tone for the excitement of this worship. Drums, trumpets, organ, orchestra, and voices gather their forces to pronounce: "*Jauchzet, frohlocket.*" The triumphant work unfolds as music director Frederick Grimes coaxes rhythm, counterpoint, melody, and meaning from the Bach score. A chorale coda quietly ends the work with Luther's Christmas hymn, "*Vom Himmel hoch.*"

Now the church is full. The candles are deliberately lighted by the acolytes. You wait again knowing this is the pattern of Christmas.

Suddenly you are alerted by a mighty roll of tympani that leads up

to a simultaneous burst of light and sound. The congregation rises in a body. The fanfare becomes the introduction to "*Adeste Fidelis*" ("O come, all ye faithful"). The singing sweeps you into the *now* of Christmas!

The choir processes down the aisle during this opening hymn and returns to the rear balcony while the white robed clergy ascend to the altar area, which is banked with Christmas trees.

The message from Scripture and from the pulpit is familiar, of course. Old accents recalled. New insights gained. Prayers. More hymns.

During the offering and during the distribution of communion, the choir, soloists, orchestra, and organ share additional musical gifts. Excerpts are offered from the *Messiah* and from Part III of *The Christmas Oratorio*.

Whatever the degree of your personal acquisition of the elements of the service at Holy Trinity, you also are tempted to see and hear and feel the experience empathetically through the senses of the others around you. They may be anonymous pilgrims like yourself, but you guess that the congregation includes professors and postmen, doctors and dowagers, jurists and journalists, rock stars and retired bankers, students and saleswomen, and sinners and saints. Among the average faces like your own, you recognize a few celebrities. Like you, they may be strangers here, too. Manhattan can be a very lonely place to be alone on Christmas Eve.

But it's almost impossible to feel sad or alone at the end of such a Christmas Eve service as this as you stand with the hundreds who have packed themselves in with you and as you take your cue from the organ and begin to sing: "Joy to the world, the Lord is come!"

Christmas in New York is a blend of many, many things. A cynic would say, "It's all show business, theatrical sham, commercial exploitation, gimmicks, hucksterism." But can't that complaint be voiced anywhere, in any city? New York has all of the people problems of the nation, perhaps of the world.

A city is people. The people in New York can't escape Christmas. Some may exploit it. Many more will celebrate it.

Photos: Macy's, New York Public Library, St. Patrick's Cathedral, Tavern on the Green, Central Park.

Symbols Tell the Christmas Story

W. A. POOVEY

A fir tree ablaze with lights, silver icicles, and brightly colored ornaments! A beautiful sight, but to many a Christmas tree is more than beauty. It represents family gatherings, reunions with wandering relatives, presents, Christmas feasts.

A red, white, and blue flag flying over a building in a foreign land. It is not just a colored banner but also a symbol of America, of freedom, of all the things we associate with the United States of America.

Symbols can be found all around us. The traffic sign is a symbol. The advertising logo is a symbol. Symbols are not only pictures; they also express abstract ideas through concrete and stylized forms.

Christians have always used symbols. The drawing of a fish served to identify a Christian home during the earliest time of persecution. This device was chosen because the Greek word for fish contained the initials for "Jesus Christ, Son of God, Savior." The cross, once an instrument of terrible punishment, is today probably the most widely known symbol in the world.

The seasons of Advent and Christmas have their symbolic language. Over the centuries artists have used symbols in carving, embroidery, and stained glass to tell the story of Christ's coming to this earth. Since Advent is closely associated with Old Testament prophecy, many Advent symbols find their origin in that section of the Bible, particularly in the book of Isaiah. Let's look at a few of Isaiah's pictures.

The rose. Isaiah 35:1 says, "The desert shall rejoice and blossom as the rose." This beautiful concept was taken as a symbol of the coming Messiah, and about the 13th century A.D. the rose became an Advent representation in church decoration. A beautiful hymn, "Lo, how a rose, e'er blooming" was written, based on this concept. The second verse is particularly meaningful.

The rose of which I'm singing
  Isaiah had foretold.
He came to us through Mary
  Who sheltered him from cold.
  Through God's eternal will
This child to us was given
  At midnight calm and still.

Strangely enough, the word in Isaiah translated "rose" isn't found in modern translations of the Bible. The Revised Standard Version and the New International Version translate the word as "crocus," the New English Bible says "asphodel," the Jerusalem Bible uses the word "jonquil," and the Good News Bible plays safe by talking about "flowers." But the symbol of a rose for the Savior still remains. Sometimes Mary is symbolized by a white rose.

The candle. The idea of light shining in darkness has always been a striking religious symbol. In our modern world we might represent this idea by an electric light bulb or a searchlight, but for people in the past a candle spoke this meaning. The book of Isaiah has two key verses that stress the idea of light. In the famous ninth chapter, which speaks about a child being born who will be called "Wonderful Counselor, Mighty God . . . " the prophet says:

The people who walked in darkness
  have seen a great light;
those who dwelt in a land of deep darkness,
  on them has light shined (Isaiah 9:2).
In Isaiah 60 the words appear:
  Arise, shine; for your light has come,

and the glory of the Lord has risen upon you.
For behold, darkness shall cover the earth,
    and thick darkness the peoples;
but the Lord will arise upon you,
    and his glory will be seen upon you.
And nations shall come to your light
    and kings to the brightness of your rising
(Isaiah 60:1-3).

It is not difficult to see how a candle symbolizes the coming of the Messiah, particularly when the idea of light infuses the opening of John's gospel: "In him was life, and the life was the light of men. The light shines in the darkness, and the darkness has not overcome it" (John 1:4-5).

The lighted candle as a symbol of the coming of Christ has been reinforced further by the use of an Advent wreath. In an Advent wreath four candles are lit, one on each Sunday in Advent. At times a fifth candle is lit on Christmas Eve to emphasize the true light which has been born.

The shoot from a stump. Isaiah 11:1 contains an interesting picture that also has become an Advent symbol. The prophet writes: "There shall come forth a shoot from the stump of Jesse, and a branch shall grow out of his roots." This idea of a branch or shoot coming forth was a popular one; Jeremiah and Zechariah both use the figure to designate the coming Messiah.

Isaiah's reference is interesting in that he begins with Jesse, David's father, rather than with the great king of

tool when there were few books and few people able to read books. The stories of David, Solomon, and others could be explained, thus the symbol provided a review of the Old Testament.

The ox and ass. One final symbol from Isaiah is worth noting. Isaiah 1:3 speaks of the ox knowing its owner and the ass knowing its master's crib. These two animals also have been used as Advent symbols. The ox was considered a symbol of patience and sacrifice; the ass represented humility and service. These were characteristics of Jesus and of his followers. Perhaps the picture of the Christ child in a manger added to the effectiveness of these animals as symbols of the Messiah. The familiar carol, "Away in a manger," refers to this with the line:

The cattle are lowing;
    The poor baby wakes,
But little Lord Jesus
    No crying he makes.

Some students of symbols decided that, in the Isaiah passage, the ox represents Israel with its Old Testament sacrifices, and the ass represents the Gentile nations in the New Testament since the ass has a cross on its shoulders and back. It is doubtful whether most of us are pleased with being represented by the ass in this symbol.

As has been indicated, Isaiah has no monopoly on Old Testament passages that refer to the Messiah. One of the most interesting messianic sections is chapters 22-24 of

Israel. Medieval stained glass artists were intrigued by the idea of a branch or shoot growing from a stump and often pictured the ancestry of Jesus in a kind of family tree, called a Jesse stem window, in the great cathedrals. York Cathedral in Northern England still has such a window. A Jesse stem window was an effective teaching

Numbers, which contains the story of that strange character Balaam. Balaam was hired by Balak, king of Moab, to curse Israel when his land was threatened by those invading hordes that had come out of Egyptian captivity. Balaam refused to say anything that the Lord didn't command him to say, and after a remarkable experience with an angel and an ass that talked to its master, the prophet finally pronounced a blessing instead of a curse on the wandering people of Israel. Included in the blessing is a picture of the Messiah using two symbols. Said Balaam:

I see him, but not now;
  I behold him, but not nigh:
a star shall come forth out of Jacob,
  and a scepter shall rise out of Israel (Numbers 24:17).

The star. The use of a star as a symbol of Jesus should not be confused with the star that led the Wise Men to the manger. That star is an Epiphany symbol and represents the coming of nations to Jesus rather than Jesus himself. But the star is a proper symbol for our Lord, for this sign is repeated at the end of the Bible where Jesus is quoted as saying, "I am the root and the offspring of David, the bright morning star" (Revelation 22:16). Anyone who has been up early enough to see a single star shining just at daybreak will know how striking this symbol is.

The scepter. The scepter is also a familiar symbol of the Messiah. We live in a day when kings no longer use such an instrument as a sign of power, except perhaps the Queen of England who does have a golden rod with a cross in diamonds and emeralds at its end. Such an instrument is a symbol of rulership, one mentioned long ago in Genesis as a messianic sign. Jacob, when blessing

The burning bush. The story of how God spoke to Moses from a burning bush told in Exodus 3 is a familiar one. By a simple association of ideas the burning bush also has become an Advent symbol, for just as God once spoke through a bush on fire, he now speaks through the newborn baby, his Son. Sometimes the bush is used as a symbol of the annunciation of the angel to Mary, for God called Mary to serve him just as he called Moses to deliver his people.

The fountain. The idea of water as a cleansing agent is stressed in the Bible, particularly in the New Testament. Baptism is a symbol of the new order; John the Baptist involved thousands in his water ritual. Later it is called the washing of regeneration. Jesus also tells the woman at the well that he can give her living water. So it isn't surprising to find an Old Testament passage that uses water to symbolize the coming Messiah. Zechariah says:

On that day, there shall be a fountain opened for the house of David and the inhabitants of Jerusalem to cleanse them from sin and uncleanness (Zechariah 13:1).

On the basis of this verse a fountain often appears as an Advent symbol, although it usually is pictured as flowing water, not as a spurt of water into the air.

The sun. John Milton wrote a famous poem called "On the Morning of Christ's Nativity." In the poem he used the sun to symbolize Christ's coming with the words,

his sons, said of Judah the ancestor of Jesus:
  The scepter shall not depart from Judah
    nor the ruler's staff from between his feet,
  until he comes to whom it belongs;
    and to him shall be the obedience of the peoples
      (Genesis 49:10).

And though the shady gloom
Had given day her room,
  The Sun himself with-held his wonted speed,
And hid his head for shame,
As his inferiour flame,
  The new enlightn'd world no more should need;

He saw a greater Sun appear
Than his bright Throne, or burning Axletree could bear.

Milton's picture was derived from the words of the Old Testament prophet Malachi who said: "But for you who hear my name the sun of righteousness shall rise, with healing in its wings" (Malachi 4:2).

Usually this symbol appears as the sun with rays extending in every direction and with the letters IHC, an abbreviation of the Greek word for Jesus, in the center. Sometimes the letters are replaced with a human face shining from the center of the sun.

When we turn to the New Testament stories of Jesus' birth, we also find symbols. Artists have often preferred to paint or carve a picture of the story rather than convey its meaning through a single symbol. But some figures or objects in the birth and annunciation stories do serve as clear signs of the deeper meaning of the coming of Christ in the world.

Angels. Heavenly messengers are involved throughout the story of the Savior's birth. Transportation between heave nand earth was crowded for a while! An angel told Zechariah in the temple that his wife would bear the forerunner, John the Baptist; an angel announced the coming of the Messiah to Mary; an angel and a whole heavenly chorus appeared to the shepherds at Jesus' birth; an angel warned Joseph in a dream to flee to Egypt. So the symbol of an angel has many meanings in con-

nection with the birth stories.

It is interesting to note what has happened to our concept of angels. The Bible says angels have no gender, but it usually pictures them as strong messengers from God. Sometimes, as in the visions of Ezekiel and Revelation, angelic beings have a strange unearthly appearance.

Gradually, however, the pictures have softened until angels are usually portrayed as soft, feminine creatures in flowing robes. They look more like birds than strong messengers. But an angel still represents good news regarding the birth of the Savior.

The manger. For anyone who knows the Christmas story as recorded in Luke 2 the manger is an easily recognized symbol. It reminds us that no place was found for the newborn king except in a stable or cave. Sometimes the manger is pictured as surrounded by a bright light, a sign of the heavenly occupant. Perhaps the bare manger is a better picture, for it reminds us of the harshness of Jesus' reception from the start of his life on earth.

Shepherd's staves or crooks. Jesus called himself the Good Shepherd, so it is only fitting that shepherds came to worship him at his birth. The visit of the shepherds often is symbolized by staves or crooks and, at times, by a lamb, since Jesus was also the Lamb of God. It is interesting to note that the Bible tells us nothing of the subsequent events in the life of the shepherds who came to the manger. Did any of them hear the Messiah when he had grown to manhood? Were any of the shepherds present at the crucifixion? The symbols only speak of the brief appearance of these people.

The coming of the magi or Wise Men provided the church with several symbols—the caskets of gold, frankincense, and myrrh, the guiding star, etc.—but these signs are a part of the Epiphany season which follows Christmas.

Two other symbols, not biblical in origin, deserve mention.

Bells. The loud sound of bells often signals the proclamation of good news. Since there is no better news for human beings than the birth of a Savior, bells are a fitting Christmas symbol. The poet Longfellow uses this symbol in a beautiful poem which begins:
I heard the bells on Christmas Day
Their old, familiar carols play,
    And wild and sweet
    The words repeat
Of peace on earth, goodwill to men!

The Glastonbury Thorn. Glastonbury near Somerset, England, is the site of an ancient monastery. According to legend, Joseph of Arimathea—the man who provided a tomb for Jesus' body—came to England in 63 A.D. to convert the people of that land. His staff, when placed in the ground, grew into a thorn tree that bloomed every Christmas. The original tree was destroyed by a fanatical Puritan, but a descendant of the original bush still stands and blooms at Glastonbury. Of course this is only a legend, but the thorn tree has become a symbol of the birth of Jesus.

Symbols, of course, cannot replace the beautiful biblical story of the coming of Jesus into this world, but they do serve as a kind of shorthand, reminding us of humankind's expectations of a Savior and the fulfilling of those expectations on that first Christmas. Our lives are enriched if we understand the symbols of Christ's coming.

The Night the Angels Sang

PHYLLIS ROOT

Quickly the word spread over the hillside.
"Angels," the grass whispered to the wind.
The wind told the thistles, huddled close to the hard ground,
and rattled the leaves of the low-lying bushes where the sparrows slept.
"Angels! Wake up," it rustled the branches.
The birds shook out their feathers and flew to tell
the leopard in her cave, the lizard under his rock.
Faster than fire the story spread.
The hare hopped timidly out of his nest.
The mice peeked out from their tunnels under the grass,
and the wild ass struggled to her feet, braying.

"Angels!" The word went round. "Not in my time
or my grandfather's time
has there been the rumor of angels."

"Not a rumor, not a rumor," rippled the grass.
"Brighter than stars, hotter than noontime,
colder than midnight, angels singing in the air."

The lion stretched, his long golden claws gleaming in the moonlight.
The hare shivered and huddled close to the brown earth.
"Where?" asked the fox, springing lightly up and down
to warm her paws, for the night was brittle cold.
"Over the hill," whispered the wind.
"Two hills, three hills, to where the sky shines
brighter than it should."
"So," hissed the snake, uncoiling from behind a rock.
"Let us go see these angels."

Slithering, creeping, crawling, leaping,
bounding, flapping, hopping, galloping,
the beasts hurried after the wind
as it flowed across the sparse grass like a river,
pointing the way.

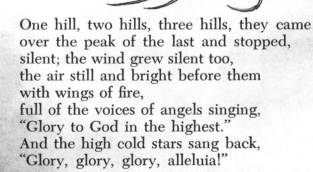

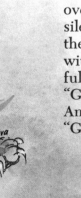

One hill, two hills, three hills, they came
over the peak of the last and stopped,
silent; the wind grew silent too,
the air still and bright before them
with wings of fire,
full of the voices of angels singing,
"Glory to God in the highest."
And the high cold stars sang back,
"Glory, glory, glory, alleluia!"

Every beast bowed its head. The hare trembled,
folding down his ears.
The wolf and the deer knelt down,
the bear crouched close to the earth,
and the badger covered his eyes with his paws.
Inside every bird and beast and insect the unearthly voices echoed:
"Peace on earth, goodwill to all."

Then the light faded, and the singing died.
In the silence they heard the trickle of a nearby spring,
fed by the winter's rain.
Below on the hillside, sheep stirred and murmured,
and the animals heard the voices of men.
"What are they saying?" the hyena asked.
"What are the men saying? What did the angels mean?"
"A child is born," whistled the wind.
"A baby is born in a manger.
They are going to find him now. They call him
'the long-awaited one.' "

"Is it the One? Is it the One?"
chittered the grasshoppers.
"The One that was promised us?" wondered the lion.
"Should he not come as a beast,
magnificent, a king, perhaps a lion?"
The hare shuddered, but the eagle flapped her wings
and spread her talons.
"He will be an eagle when he comes," she retorted.
"Soaring over heaven and earth, lord above all."
"No, no, a mouse," the tiny creatures squeaked.
But the hare said in a small voice,
"I think we should follow the shepherds
and see why the angels sang."

The grass nodded in agreement.
The animals fell silent
and started down the hill, keeping to the shadows.
The hare stayed carefully away from the bright teeth and claws
of the bear and the lion and the wolf.
But they padded ahead, intent on the journey.
The gazelle picked up her feet with care for the smaller animals
scurrying beneath her.
The tortoise lumbered behind, puffing, "Wait for me, wait for me."

The shepherds hurried along, down the hill to where
the buildings of a city lay scattered like fallen stars.
On the outskirts they stopped, before a run-down stable.
"See," muttered the owl. "A stable. It must be a beast after all."
"Shhh," hissed the snake.

From the stable door a light gleamed,
brighter than the wings of angels,
warmer than the morning sun.
The shepherds disappeared inside.

Silently the animals crowded closer,
peering through the windows and door
and through the wide cracks in the walls.
Inside, a tired donkey munched hay.
Sheep and oxen nestled in the straw.
All of them—donkey, sheep, cattle, shepherds—
gazed at the manger where a newborn child lay,
with a man and a woman watching tenderly over him.
A look of peace filled the eyes of all,
as though they too had heard the angels sing.

The hare's ears twitched. Never had he seen anything so wonderful.
All his life he had feared human beings
and the hurt they could do him.
But somehow he knew that the baby meant him no harm.
He took a timid hop into the stable, then another, and another.
Closer and closer he hopped, till the woman saw him and smiled.
"Come, little bunny,"
she held out her hands, and he hopped into them.
The woman stroked his long brown ears, and he quivered once, then lay still.
Gently she laid him in the hay, next to the sleeping child.
His whiskers tickled the baby's face.
He opened his eyes and smiled.

One by one, the other beasts crept into the stable.
Even when the lion came forward and knelt on the ground,
the sheep and oxen showed no fear.
Then, one by one, they slipped out again into the night.
The hare was the last to go, hopping down from the straw.

Outside, the others were waiting for him.
Slowly they started back up the hill.
Grey streaked the eastern edge of the sky,
and morning was close at hand.
"It was him, wasn't it?" the lion said at last,
in a deep rumbling voice.
"The long-awaited one," replied the falcon, flapping her wings.
"Not a beast at all," squeaked a mouse.
"He sent his own son," the porcupine said softly.
"What greater promise could he give?"

One last star still burned brightly as they drifted away,
all to their own homes.
The hare paused at the top of the hill to watch it shining.
Faintly he heard again the cold bright singing of the stars.
"Peace on earth," he whispered to himself.
And the wind whispered back, "Peace."
Then the hare flicked his ears
and hopped away into the high grass.

Our Christmas

Christmas Eve _____
_____

Christmas Day _____
_____

Christmas Worship _____
_____

Christmas Guests

_____
_____
_____
_____
_____
_____
_____
_____
_____

Christmas
Photo

Christmas Gifts

_____
_____
_____
_____
_____
_____
_____
_____
_____